From Fear to Freedom

The events of this book occurred between 1940 and 1970 as reported through letters, stories, and memories of individuals who lived through them.

Author: Jamey Dye

Table of Contents

Forward

This book was not my idea. I visited Hap Skinner in Cairns, Australia on my return from Wagu Village in 2012. Hap urged me to write down the story of the Wagu people and their relationship to Wayne and Sally. He spoke with an intensity that inspired me. That began a journey that ended with this book. I am a better human because of Hap's words and his life.

I want to thank the people of Wagu for welcoming our family into their tribe. For generously sharing their food, time, energy, and love. The grace with which they embrace adversity has been a lifelong inspiration to me. Their strength, courage, generosity continue to challenge me in the execution of my life.

I want to thank my parents, Wayne and Sally Dye for providing the letters and reports from their files. They were passionately committed to truth and to making sure their story included their failures, frustrations, and internal relational struggles. Thank you for your love, hard work, and passion.

I want to thank Tina, Edie, and Abby for stepping in at the last minute to polish it off. Without them it would have been a much less polished work.

I would like to thank my children Matthew and Shannon Dye for working with me on message and content. They worked long hours on the book and inspired me to get the story right.

I would like to thank my dear wife Cheryl for being patient with me as I worked on this over the past five years.

My hope is that you will find this true story impactful on your life journey as you seek to explore true reality and how it impacts your community.

Jamey Dye

6

Prologue:

Young Naba awoke to the sound of bat wings, the all-too-familiar flapping of thieves, as it slowed to grab a Malay apple from the tree outside. His stomach growled; he had combed that tree for a long time yesterday looking for fruit. How did the bat find what he could not? He gained a new respect for the creature and its ability to find food, and resolved to look harder next time. He lay there listening to the early morning sounds of the jungle and wondering where he would get his next meal. Dawn had not yet come, but already the day birds were calling; the night insects and frog noises were quieting in anticipation of the new day.

Still lying there, planning the day's food supply, he tried to remember the last time he had actually felt full. It had been over a month since any hunter had brought a pig into the village. The dry season had allowed the pigs to fan out across the marshes of the Sepik plane, making them almost impossible to find or catch. There were fish and he was a good fisherman, but he did not have a canoe, so he was forced to work from the banks. His spear, a long slender shaft of black palm, had been broken and repaired so often it had shrunk to half its original size. He could not throw it into the deep channels or it would sink to the bottom, completely unrecoverable. He went back over the routes he had taken over the past several weeks, trying to remember something he had missed. Had he overlooked a pocket of bush or tree that might hold something to eat? Was there a log full of grubs he had not noticed? His empty stomach ached as he rolled over and tried to go back to sleep, but he knew it was hopeless.

Naba slapped at a mosquito and peered through a crack in the floor of the house, trying to judge if it was light enough to chase away the spirits so he could start his daily hunt for food. The light gave him courage to consider a venture further into the jungle where his late father had not taken him before. He had now lived through eight *kiya* seasons when a delicious palm fruit becomes ripe and feasting begins. Most children did not live to be as old as he was now. The men said women in enemy villages sent the evil *kwonu* spirits to kill them. The babies had been particularly vulnerable. But the evil spirits did not get Naba. Before his passing, his father had encouraged him, "Be strong. Don't be afraid. I am going to the great fire. My *dafa* spirit will stay near and protect you. When you are older, you can learn the rituals from Uncle Naintu to call me to come into you and give you power to heal people." Naba clung to these memories of his father, Basuwi Sawini, the only person in his memory who had loved and cared for him. He died protecting the family from their invading neighbors. Naba had not known his mother, Kamei. Family told him the *kwonu* killed her soon after he was born.

Remembering his father gave Naba incentive to get up from his mat and prepare for the daily hunt. He reached for his small string bag and felt through the woven fabric for the most important items: the cassowary leg bone dagger from his father, a carving tool made from a large rodent tooth, three shells, and a roll of banana leaves he had picked in the garden. The spear hidden outside, held power from his father's *dafa* spirit to help him hunt. The rodent tooth was the hardest and sharpest thing he had, and he used it to dig into wood and to sharpen his spear.

Naba slipped off his mat quietly, holding his string bag. He did not want to awaken his uncle, Kwiba Sawini, or aunt, Wama, who slept beyond the stone and clay fire platform. On this side of the platform slept his younger uncle Naintu, a full-grown man who did not have a wife yet. Cousin Ginwa also slept near

2

Naba, but the boy was too young to go with him on this adventure. Naba carefully worked his way around them and stepped between the family's hunting dogs sleeping by the fire pit until he was near enough to reach the smoking coals.

He pulled his dried tobacco leaf off the drying shelf above the fire pit and rolled it in a dried banana leaf he drew from his bag before slinging it over his shoulder. Then, Naba grabbed a smoldering stick to light his homemade cigar-like his father had taught him. He added a log to the fire so some smoke would continue to bring enough warmth to his family, allowing them to sleep comfortably without any covering on their woven mat. The smoke also helped rid the air of mosquitoes, while the woven mat kept them from biting through the holes in the bark floor.

His preparations finished, Naba headed for the small patch of light along the palm stem wall and stepped high over the wide palm bark acting as a door. It kept out the neighbor's dogs and other wild animals. Naba had been taught that it would also keep out the wandering spirits.

When out on the ledge at the entryway, Naba reached up and carefully removed his spear from under the roof thatching. Then he prepared to descend the six feet from the house platform resting on forked posts buried deep in the ground. Six tall forked posts held up the roof cross bars and thatch. Carefully tied vines held everything in place. He lowered the four-inch diameter log notched for footholds which acted as the stairway. Oops! One of his uncle's mangy older dogs looked up briefly from his guard spot curled up under the house. Naba feared he might howl and wake everyone, but the dog recognized him and put his head back down.

Naba quietly made his way between the stilted thatch houses, clustered together for protection against raids from other tribes. He did not want to awaken his many relatives still sleeping, five to ten people covering the bark floor in each house. Some were related by birth, others were in-laws, and many were adopted in, given kin names and interacted with as if they were real blood relatives. Loosely-kept agreements between leading men kept the family groups together.

Naba stopped by the small stream near the edge of the village and drank deeply before turning and heading into the rainforest. As he looked at the shadows in the forest, he wondered if he had gotten up too early. Had the night spirits gone to bed yet? But his hunger was stronger than his fear, and he headed quickly down the path. His callused bare feet slapped quietly on the bare worn earth, and the cool morning felt good. His toes dug in on the slippery spots, instinctively avoiding the thorns and broken tree stumps along the way.

As he distanced himself from the village, the signs of the trail grew fainter and fainter, and the forest grew thicker and darker. Soon he was no longer following a path, but rather a route; he stopped to listen as leaves rustled. Each rustle was different, and he could usually tell without looking what creature made each sound. Most of the sounds came from small rats and lizards and large insects.

A flapping startled him. Naba swore under his breath, "Big fire." He had scared off a Victoria Crowned Pigeon. He was angry that he had not heard it before it flew. The five-pound bird was easy to kill and made an excellent meal. He slowed down and concentrated on making less noise. He came across a fallen log and noticed some fresh sawdust on the ground. Breakfast at last. Grabbing his rodent tooth from his bag, he began to scrape away the rotting bark. His fingers began to ache from the pressure, but he was making progress. He saw the white segmented body of a two-inch-long horn beetle larva trying to burrow deeper into the log. He used his dagger to stab the wood just ahead of it to block its escape. Then, carefully, he scraped away the last of the wood and gently pulled the larva from the log. Once he had the larva in his hands, he bit its head and popped it into his mouth. He had learned the hard way never to put beetle larva in his mouth without first crushing the head with his teeth. They bite back—hard. He was able to extract four more grubs over the course of the next 45 minutes, and, as he ate them, his stomach gradually began to stop hurting.

He was now further in the forest than he had ever been in this direction. His decision to ignore his family's warnings about the spirits off this way was paying off with some food, but he still worried.

He rested for a moment and listened to the woods, wondering which way to go next. He heard water trickling over rocks and followed the sound to a small overgrown spring. As he pulled away the vines for a drink, he discovered a small cluster of edible water bulbs to finish off his morning snack; he dug those out of the tangle of roots with the butt of his spear. Now that his stomach had stopped aching with hunger, his mind began to wander back into fear. He wondered if he had offended any of the *wulyal* that his father said created and guarded various parts of land everywhere. *Wulyal* tended to live in springs, waterfalls or unusual land formations. They could cause sickness, but not usually death.

Naba began to ponder this as he turned back toward the village. He could easily retrace his steps, but a part of him ached to see more. A noise above him caught his attention; he turned back on full alert. The spring was coming out of the side of a steep slope, and above, he could hear the steady rustling sound of a

5

wallaby.

As quietly as he could, he began to ascend the slope, trying to avoid any brush that would rustle above him. One of the few things his father had taught him before he died was how to avoid brushing against young saplings. When you bump a young sapling at the base, the leaves above announce your presence.

After 100 yards of creeping up the side of the mountain he was still no closer to his prey. It seemed to stay just far enough ahead, like it knew he was there. He crept faster, hoping to make ground. He strained with all of his senses to locate the wallaby; he could smell it now and knew it was almost within spear range. Naba crested a ridge, arm pulled back and ready to throw. He got a glimpse and chucked his spear just as the little creature saw him and bolted into the thicket. He knew as his spear left his hand that it was a bad throw, but he froze, hopeful that just maybe it would find its mark. As the spear disappeared into the dense brush beyond his fleeing prey, Naba cursed. Behind the location where the wallaby had been standing was "huba," a dense crush of jungle vegetation that was sometimes impossible to negotiate. When a large tree fell in the jungle, it would drag all the smaller trees and vines with it. They would lie crushed beneath the big tree in a collection so thick it was impossible to get through.

Naba pushed his way into the huba, letting his eyes adjust to the dark underbrush, praying his spear was not lost forever. Straining as hard as he could past the heavy branches in front of him, he was able to just reach the very tip of his spear handle, buried in the dense brush in front of him. He tugged with his fingers and slowly pulled the spear backwards out of the tangle. Exhausted from the struggle of the hunt and the climbing, he slumped down on one of the large branches protruding from the huba and caught his breath.

The sound of his pulse was slowly subsiding in his head when he noticed that above the huba was a large tear in the jungle canopy. The log he was sitting on was a branch from the large tree that had ripped the hole. He climbed up the branch and the rest of the tree into the light above. Naba found himself standing up high and looking out through the hole in the jungle onto an incredible scene.

He could see the thin black ribbon of a stream that wound past his village. He recognized the trees near the mouth of the small tributary his village, Namu, was on. He followed the black ribbon and saw off in the distance a large silver flat object surrounded by jungle mountains on one side and green grassy swamp on the other. In the distance, right near the horizon, he saw a thin sliver of brown. As the clouds shifted and the sun glinted on the brown ribbon, he recognized it as a large far-away river.

He had heard of the mighty Sepik River, a mile wide in places, but he had never seen it. He had also heard of a large lake, but he had never seen that either. Naba wondered at the world before him as he looked out at that lake and far away at the Sepik River. He looked past them at the mountains that rose into the clouds and out of sight and wondered if they ever ended. The world around appeared suddenly bigger; his world around the village seemed suddenly smaller. His heart skipped. He had hope for the first time since his father died—a little sliver of hope that maybe he could make a way in the world beyond the places he was seeing. He knew he needed something more than going through each day half starved, struggling to find his next meal.

Chapter 1 – Wagu Village

The Sepik River, the largest in northern New Guinea, is a key geological and socio-political feature on the island. After World War I, Australian veterans took control of the plantations and lands owned by the German Empire and the German New Guinea Company. In support of these plantation owners, the Australian government began to establish administrative control in the east Sepik valley using government paid officers called Kiaps, but generally these Kiaps kept to the navigable water of the Sepik River. In 1941 the Empire of Japan invaded the Sepik River valley, and it remained under Japanese control until the end of World War II in 1945. After the War, the plantations and the government resumed their management of the valley.

The plantation owners took advantage of the government's control of the Sepik River to recruit laborers from the people they encountered. The recruiters would travel with a team of New Guinea national employees trying to find "fresh kanakas" (unacculturated people) for contract labor on the plantations. The recruiters went to remote places to collect young men who knew nothing about money or Western culture. They intentionally avoided taking on too many people from a single language group to avoid the possibility of them understanding each other and rising up against them. These young men had no understanding of labor laws. They were employed primarily to climb the coconut trees and pick coconuts, break and dry them. It was an exploitive environment, but it had improved from the pre-War practices of flogging as punishment for minor infractions. The plantation owners typically paid these workers in rations and a small amount of spending money, along with a relatively big sum when the contract was finished.

Government control of the valley made some of the people of Namu feel safe enough to establish the village of Yigai in order to access better fishing and Western technology. Yigai was on a little sliver of land that extended like an arm from the foothills of the Hunstein Mountain Range. The village was perched on a high point of land on the edge of the Hunstein River, which flows to the Sepik. Naba Sawini responded readily when the recruiters arrived in the village of Yigai. His lack of immediate family, the daily struggle for food, and the lure of Western technology were enough to motivate him to leave his village and try his luck at the plantation. It is likely that his cousins Ginwa and Bogo joined him.

On the plantation, the young men learned to use knives, axes, matches, metal pots, machetes, fishing line and hooks, and metal spear tips. They learned to speak Tok Pisin, a trade language made up of local words mixed with some English and German words. They learned what books were and had a glimpse into the larger world through stories from others and observing their Australian overlords. The plantation workers lived in commune-style homes made mostly from local materials. At the end of their contracts, they were able to exchange their wages for tools and clothing for their relatives. When plantation workers were returned to their villages, their new goods gave them more negotiating power than young people were expected to have, since sharing generously with others is the focal source of prestige in their culture.

Map of South Pacific showing New Guinea

When Naba returned to Yigai, he felt like he was no longer a needy little boy, but a young man with powerful tools and useful knowledge. After the plantation, Naba returned to Naintu's house with several other young men and women. One of these was another young orphan named Yasiyo. Naintu had married Kaba, a barren widow of a relative. (Local custom required all widows to marry clan members since the bride price had been paid by contributions from that clan.) As a married man, Naintu Sawini was the head of his house. It was common for young men like Naba to live in the home of a married man and help him hunt and fish. The young men provided protection as well.

The people of Yigai village spoke the language of the Gahom people, one of the many language groups in the foothills of the Hunstein Mountain Range. Thanks to the men returning from the plantation, they also began to learn some Tok Pisin.

11

Wagu Lake is a large lake a four-hour canoe ride upriver from Yigai village. Highly valued fish, saltwater crocodiles, ducks, and waterlily thrived in the lake. Rare exotic birds, lizards, snakes, wild pigs and cassowaries filled the forest around the lake. It was a perfect place to hunt and gather. Food was plentiful. Several villages had access to the lake and the surrounding swamp in this Sepik River floodplain. Although Wagu Lake was highly valued, it was little used because of fear of being killed by neighboring tribes.

East Sepik traditional people killed for a variety of reasons, including stealing, rape, revenge after a man died, and even someone wandering into the wrong territory. There were also more exotic reasons, such as sorcery and gaining power from people by eating them. The book *Savage Harvest: A Tale of Cannibals, Colonialism, and Michael Rockefeller's Tragic Quest for Primitive Art* concludes that Rockefeller was killed and eaten for his power. Regardless of the cause, raiding and killing were common practices among these Sepik peoples.

The villages in the region with potential access to the lake included Namu and Yigai, Yambun and Malu, Brugnowi, and Genesowayagu. Each spoke a different language. Yambun and Malu spoke Manambu, Brugnowi spoke Abelam, Genesowayagu spoke its own language, unique to that village, and Yigai and Namu spoke Gahom. Gahom was a village on the other side of the Hunstein Mountain Range.

These numerous and diverse people groups did not understand each other. They lived in fear of each other and of the spirits in the forest. As a result, these communities, separated by their varying local languages, fought and killed each other regularly.

Sometime in the late 1940s or early 1950s the Yambun people and the Genesowayagu people decided to stop fighting over

Wagu lake and make peace. It is not clear why these two people groups decided to make an agreement regarding these lakes and swamps. Some contributing factors may have been growing knowledge of the trade language; the Catholic Mission moving into Ambunti at the center of the Manambu area; and Australian government efforts to make peace after the Japanese were overcome. The goal of the treaty was to allow mutual fishing and hunting rights in and around Wagu Lake. The deal was a rare example of tribal cooperation. It was established with a "breaking of arrows" ceremony and a feast. Both tribes have honored the treaty over the years.

In this agreement, the Yambuns and the Genesowayagus could fish and hunt freely on Wagu Lake. However, the Yambuns could only build on the hills along the Hunstein River adjacent to the lake. The Genesowayagu people could build their houses anywhere on the lake itself without fearing reprisal from the Yambun people. The Genesowayagus started by creating a few temporary shelters for occasional hunting and gathering trips. The Genesowayagu people had lived in the foothills north of Mt. Hunstein along the Hunstein River as long as they could remember. Their village population was likely around 25 to 35 people, the average for villages throughout the Sepik forests. The river and forests provided an abundance of food. Yet, too many people were dying before they saw their children mature. Few children survived. These people believed that all deaths were caused by other people in other tribal groups. There could be no natural deaths in their view of the world. Every time an adult died, the spiritual leaders had to use divining techniques to discover who caused it. A dream could be enough to confirm that an enemy was the cause of someone's death.

Sometime in the early 1950s the Genesowayagu people decided to attack the people of Yessan village. It is speculated that they were convinced the Yessans had caused the recent deaths. The

Genesowayagu people walked for several days to reach Yessan. They raided the village, killing as many as they could. The Yessans fought back and none of the Genesowayagu men who went on the raid survived.

It is not clear why the Yessans were so effective in the defense, but we do know that 10 years earlier the Yessan people were rewarded handsomely with axes, knives, and machetes by the Australian commandos for helping them evade the Japanese in a covert mission to blow up weapons supplies in Wewak. The book *Wewak Mission* by Lionel Veale is a fascinating account of one of the many battles fought in North Eastern New Guinea during World War II. It is possible that the weapons given to the Yessan people by the commandos turned the tide in the battle against the Genesowayagu invaders. As a result of the raid, the majority of the men who spoke the Genesowagu language were wiped out.

Yafei Tuhiyu did not participate in the raid. When the men did not return, Yafei, one of the last remaining men in the village, stepped up as tribal leader. He took responsibility for the men, women, and children that were left behind. Yafei found his village vulnerable to invasion and sorcery.

We don't know much about Yafei as a child or young man but we do know he was a survivor. His mother had trained him to take matters into his own hands to do whatever it took to move forward. He did describe his father as a violent man. So violent, in fact, that his mother convinced him and his siblings to wait in ambush along the trail for their father and kill him. The family made a fire and cooked and ate parts of him, including his brains to gain his power for the next generation.

Yagumei - Yafei's wife after the raid

Families who joined Yafei in Wagu :

- Wanegi arrived with his wife, Mongwi, and accepted Batko as his second wife.

- Bagi had two wives, Mali with her daughter Dwali and Maki from the village of Nikilu with her adopted daughter Bayei. Several younger men came with them: Wafiyo Dehi with his wife Faisowa, Magofa, and Begai Wuna.

- Kedul arrived in Wagu with three wives . Bagu came with her daughters Sufa and Bowi; Midi brought her sons Wamini and Wabuwa; Doma brought her daughter Moyali and adopted son Leito.

In his first act of leadership, Yafei took Yagumei, the widow of the previous tribal leader, as his wife. He established a village site on the lake and called it Wagu. He then set out to recruit men to help protect his village and his land.

Yafei's only resource was the other widows after the raid. He offered them as peace makers to men from nearby villages. He also promised the remaining younger girls as future wives. Part of this agreement was that the men would come and live at Wagu. Most of

15

the women went along with his plan, but some chose to flee to distant villages for safety. When Yafei approached the village of Yigai, he offered his sister Yamu as a bride for a man who would come to live in Wagu. The man, Naintu, agreed. He was hoping Yamu would be able to have children, since his other wife Kaba was barren. Naba, Ginwa, and Yasiyo followed Naintu to Wagu.

Yafei recruited men from Gahom, Nikilu, and Kakilu to rebuild the village. Bagi and Wanegi Hubafu were mature men who came from Gahom to take new wives in Wagu.

Kedul of Kakilu wanted to take advantage of Yafei's offer. In order to cross Nikilu land to come to Wagu, he arranged to have a peace child given to Nikilu. The baby, Kokomo, was given to Kikwali Wabufayo. All these people enlarged the Wagu Village population to around thirty.

To the east Sepik people in general and the Wagu people specifically, the spirit world is as real as, if not more real than the physical world. For the Wagu people the three principal types of supernatural beings are the _kwonu_, kwonu, and dafa.

Wulyal are creator spirits who live in rocks, deep pools, and on cliffs. Each clan has its own _wulyal_. Each village has several who live in the land belonging to it and validate the village's claim to the land. Each _wulyal_ has a specific abode, such as a rock cliff. These _wulyal_ were living before first people, and were considered responsible for the origin of people, for some land features, for the origin of mosquitos (by accident), and for some cultural objects. The _wulyal_ also imparted spiritual knowledge to the ancestors. _Wulyal_ are believed to control the supply of wild pigs, making them appear in front of hunters. Active following of the spiritual traditions and practices pleases the _wulyal_, and they reward people with success in many kinds of activities.

Kwonu spirits are essentially evil; they cause almost all deaths except homicides. They can be chased away by certain curers, but otherwise cannot be resisted. They are powerful and require powerful magic to defeat. Fear of the *kwonu* drives many actions and ways of thinking in Wagu culture. The Wagu people believe death always has a cause. If it is not an obvious physical cause, it is a spiritual cause, but they believe there is always a human being, most often a woman controlling who they kill.

Yafei performing spirit ceremonies

Dafa is the term for the spirit of a human or animal. An animal's *dafa* goes to an unknown place when the animal dies. A person's "true self" is the person's *dafa*, which lives inside his body while he or she is alive. When the individual dies, the *dafa* leaves his or her body. These *dafa* no longer inside human bodies could be called upon by curers to heal most diseases and help fight sorcerers. However, the Wagu people did not see them as having much power over *kwonu*—although some still hoped they did. *Dafa* were not always helpful: A *dafa* of a man recently killed could return to a village and haunt it. The *dafa* could cause mischief and even had the power to kill someone to avenge his own death or the death of a relative.

While the village was growing from immigrants, a disturbingly large number of adults and children were dying. As the village leader, Yafei could not understand the cause of these deaths, and he began to seek the *dafa* and *wulyal* for help.

The men in the village built a house of worship (called a Tamberan House) to please the *wulyal* and *dafa*. The men crafted spirit carvings, and performed rituals to infuse them with spiritual power. They crafted 10 to 12 foot-long bamboo pipes with a deep bass sound and played them to appeal to the *wulyal* spirits, hoping they would provide protection from the evil *kwonu*. The women and children had to hide when the *wulyal* came to the spirit house. Only the men could enter the place where the instruments and carved faces of the *wulyal* were played and stored. Men told the women and children that the *wulyal* made the beautiful music, but the hoarseness of the men's voices revealed the truth to astute spouses.

At the time when the kiya fruit came ripe, signaling the New Year or Kiyamogu, the whole village sang songs to praise all the things the *wulyal* had created. It took at least three full nights to perform all the songs to each created plant or animal in the villagers' world. The people made new clothing of bush materials, decorated their bodies, and made elaborate headdresses to participate in this song fest. Yafei led the people to worship in this way, hoping that the *wulyal* spirits would grant them more food and protection.

As people continued to die, Yafei intensified his attempts to please the Spirits. The village began strictly enforcing old traditions about food restrictions for women and children. Small infants and toddlers were restricted to milk and small portions of dry sago. As soon as a child reached puberty the diet was changed to a strict regimen of sago and greens, especially during the coming of age rituals.

Food taboos for pregnant women were even more restrictive.

Nursing mothers also had strong limitations. Meat, fish and other protein foods were not allowed for pregnant or nursing women, nor were most fruits and vegetables. The Wagu people considered some foods, like the brains of an enemy, especially power-giving. Only men were allowed to eat such foods. Likewise, only old people past fertility were allowed to eat eggs. When a person died, no one ate until after the burial.

Naba was a sensitive man, and he knew there was something wrong. He prayed to the spirits for answers.

Historical Note:

No records have been found of the first contact with the villages of Yigai or Wagu by the Australian government. We do know that the government officers in Ambunti were aware of them by 1962. The Wagu people were not considered a tribe or language group by the government until the discovery of Gahom village in 1963 (Spelled G'hom by the reporting patrol officer or *"Kiap"* J.O. Hunter). There was a man from Wagu on the 1963 Hunter Expedition up the April River. Hunter describes the people as follows:

"A group of over one hundred semi-nomadic people living in an isolated area between two mountain ranges south of Ambunti has been contacted by a Native Affairs patrol led by Patrol Officer J.O. Hunter.

Known as the G'hom [Gahom] people they hunt and wander over a large area of land between the Hunstein Range and the Double Mountain range south of the Sepik River. Their existence was previously unknown to the Administration, and to all but a few of the Middle Sepik people."

Hunter's description of the people and their culture included the following excerpts:

Inside [the men's house there were] spears, bows and arrows and bone knives. Also hidden there were carved and painted wooden shields about 6' long and 3' wide; human "stick" figures, painted mainly in yellow, red and white; also bamboo flutes and small carved figures. A few skulls were partially buried in the earthen floor."

"They are still using stone axes, the only steel seen being a single rusty old bush knife, a couple of cheap sheath-knives, and a large piece of metal from a wrecked wartime airplane"

The University of California, San Diego recently published online archives of the Australian "kiaps" (government officers) from the mid-1930s onward. The full record of the discovery of Gahom Village can be found in these archives.

The government's contact with Gahom Village in 1963 defined Gahom as a people group and was the beginning of a relationship with the west that would have a significant impact on both the Gahom and the Wagu people.

Chapter 2 - Wayne's Early Years

Marion Dye, Wayne's father, was the oldest of five children. His parents were Florence and Winfred, his brothers were Cecil and Robert, and his sisters were Bertha and Grace. His father was a carpenter in a small south Texas town. Winfred left Florence when Marion was around 14. When Winfred left, Florence brought the family to Michigan. There, Marion became a major breadwinner for his family by working as a carpenter.

Florence raised her children to be passionate about evangelical missions. All of her children spent their adult lives in mission work. She remained active in a mission of her own until she grew too old to travel. Once her children were grown and out of the house, she would pick a city from a map. She traveled there and found work as a housekeeper or maid. Then she visited the local churches until she found one that she felt was preaching the Gospel and nurturing believers. An acceptable church, in Florence's mind, had to preach from the Bible on Sunday mornings, have a Sunday night service, and have a Wednesday night prayer meeting. Once she found the church, Florence walked from door to door after work each day, inviting people to attend the church. Each year she picked a new city or town to live and work in. This was her way of spreading the Gospel.

Cecil and Robert were the most famous family members. Cecil cofounded New Tribes Mission. He rallied a team of six men and their families to reach a remote tribe in Bolivia in January 1944. Cecil and Robert's trip to Bolivia was the organization's first mission trip.

Five of the men on the trip were ambushed and killed while trying to reach a remote tribe, the Ayores. Robert and Cecil were among those killed. The following is one of Cecil's final letters:

21

A Call for "All Out" Volunteers:

I don't believe we care so much whether this expedition is a failure so far as our lives are concerned, but we want God to get the most possible glory from everything that happens, and we know that the powers of Hell are marshalled against anything that would bring about this desired aim. On the other hand, it seems that it would be a real testimony to the Lord's power to make this expedition successful. Then again, perhaps, more Christians would become more aware of their responsibility to lost men and less concerned over the material things of this life if the expedition failed and we lost our lives. Maybe, they would pray more for the next group that went to the same tribe, and, maybe, there would be more "all out" volunteers so that every tribe would be reached in our generation. I believe the real attitude of every fellow in this group is that they want, at any cost, that which will glorify God most.

Cecil Dye

"*. . . as my Father hath sent me, even so send I you.*" John 20:21

Wayne was nine when he first heard the news that they were missing. Not long after this, the organization sent out the letter. The impact on Wayne was profound. He had looked up to Cecil and Robert and had seen their effective ministry in central Michigan. The family had talked about them around the dinner table and prayed for them while they were on the trip. He was awed by their commitment, but perplexed by the way they had attempted to contact extremely hostile people.

A few years later the only remaining male missionary, Joe Moreno, did succeed in befriending the Ayore people by a

L-R David Bacon, Cecil Dye, George Hosbach, Robert Dye Eldon Hunter

method he seems to have invented, involving successive giving, then exchanges of practical gifts. Wayne was impressed with his wisdom and commitment. Moreno would become one of the few men Wayne idealized. .A detailed account of this story can be found in the book *God Planted Five Seeds* by Jean Dye Johnson

Marion was a hard worker. He worked as a carpenter by day and did mission work in the evenings and weekends. His intense drive to fully obey what he read in the Bible was influenced by the contrast between his mother's humble service and the casual way his father had interpreted Christianity to allow many different lifestyles, including serial adultery.

Marion met Edith Trueman in Wyandotte, Michigan. Both of them felt that God wanted them to devote their lives to the task of telling others about Jesus. Even before they were married they wanted to discover God's will and attended Nyack Bible Institute.

Early in their marriage Edith and Marion traveled as missionaries. Marion would often insist that they leave their young son

Douglas with family or friends while they went on evangelistic trips around the U.S.

Later, they felt God sending them to the Appalachian mountain people of Kentucky. It was in the mountains of Kentucky in 1935 that their second son, Wayne, was born. In those days the Appalachians were a rough place to live. They were often hungry; when Edith became pregnant she feared her baby would be brain damaged from malnutrition. After enduring hardship for five years, the family finally became so sick, so starving, and so cold that she believed they were all going to die. Edith remembers being very weak, losing all hope, and crying out to God with what she thought was her dying breath. Her next memory was of a neighbor banging on the door and coming in to feed and take care of them.

When they recovered, the family went to Michigan, where Marion went back to being a carpenter instead of a missionary. This seeming failure was difficult for them to overcome, and they remained passionate about missions and outreach and instilled that passion in Wayne.

During World War II both Marion and Edith worked for the war effort. Edith worked as a factory guard and Marion worked as a master carpenter making wooden molds for the bombers. Edith always treasured a Plexiglas cross Marion made for her from scraps of Plexiglas from his work.

Edith and Marion raised their children to work hard also. While both of his parents worked, Wayne collected tin foil and scrap metal and turned it in as his way of supporting the war effort. Later he and his brother sold papers. The boys gave half the money to their mom and kept half for themselves.

Wayne often tells a story, a lesson in character, from his boyhood. He brought a can of milk home from an army barracks where he was selling newspapers. He had grabbed it off the store shelf without paying for it. He had seen soldiers do this, and it seemed like a way to supply food for the family. His dad questioned him about where he got the milk. After his description of how he obtained it, Marion scolded Wayne for stealing and hauled him back to the barracks that same evening to return the milk and apologize to the base commander. The memory of his father's strong reaction instilled in him the idea that always doing right was absolutely mandatory.

Marion's sister Grace and her husband, Wilfred Gulick, were missionaries in Haiti. They often returned to Michigan on breaks. Wayne became a Christian as a young boy and worked in an inner city church his dad pastored. He loved the days when his Aunt Grace would visit. Wayne would help her with church meetings by running films of their work in Haiti on the movie projector while Grace stood at the front of the room narrating. During one of these sessions, his aunt read the scripture "the harvest is plentiful but the workers are few." Wayne thought for the first time, "I will go, Lord." He recalls being about age fourteen at the time.

Wayne's Aunt Dorothy, who was Cecil Dye's widow, was a missionary in South America with her three children. As her two daughters grew older, they were no longer safe in the area she was working in as a missionary, so she sent them back to live with Edith and Marion. These girls, Betty and Kay, became like sisters to Wayne.

One day Wayne was on his way to the store to buy supplies for a dollhouse for the girls. A drunk driver struck Wayne from behind. Edith heard Wayne screaming five blocks away and came running while witnesses called an ambulance. Wayne legs were crushed beneath the tires of the car.

Following this accident, Wayne was strung up in traction in the county hospital for three months. The timing of the severe injury during his junior high growing years made Wayne physically awkward. On top of that his high intellectual abilities made him a social outcast among his peers in both Junior

When Wayne was ready to graduate from high school, he told his family and church friends his next step would be the six-month New Tribes Mission training camp. His parents surprised him by saying it was too soon; Wayne was only sixteen, not ready yet for the challenge of missions. As he pondered

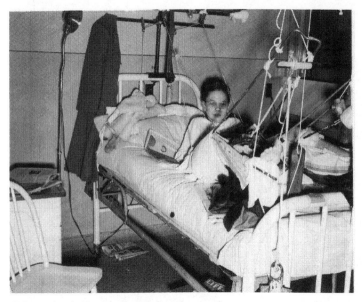

Wayne in the hospital with legs in traction

what to do instead, a teacher friend challenged him to go to college. She said he needed to train his mind and that he would be a better missionary if he got a college degree. He took her advice and began looking at colleges. His parents and his Aunt Grace were concerned that if he went to state university, they would fill his head with humanistic ideas and he would lose his faith. They began trying to find ways to finance Wayne's education at Wheaton College near Chicago. However, Wheaton only taught liberal arts, and Wayne wanted to learn something more scientific and practical.

He eventually applied for and received an academic scholarship to the University of Michigan. The academic scholarship, combined with a few thousand dollars that eventually came through from a civil suit against the drunk driver who had hit him in junior high, along with part-time work and what his parents could afford to contribute, enabled Wayne to study at the university. Wayne started out in aerospace engineering, but soon discovered it was all about designing planes, not useful for flying them. He switched to civil engineering, because he believed it would be more practical on the mission field.

The University of Michigan's chapter of InterVarsity Christian Fellowship (IVCF) was truly a life changing experience for Wayne. Because of his dad's narrow-minded views, he had been isolated from the larger context of Christian culture. The members of IVCF were enthusiastic about their faith; they were generally non-denominational in their thinking; they were deep-thinking intellectuals and had grown up with a broad set of backgrounds. At InterVarsity he found Christian friends with whom he could openly discuss variant evangelical Christian viewpoints.

Wayne embraced InterVarsity with whole-hearted enthusiasm. In addition to regularly attending Grace Bible Church, an evangelical church near the university, he attended a Sunday afternoon program, a Friday evening group meeting, a weekly dorm Bible study, and a daily after-school prayer session. He also went to Fall and Spring retreats and an InterVarsity summer camp his sophomore year. Unfortunately, InterVarsity Christian Fellowship became such a large part of Wayne's life that it took too much time away from his school work, and as a result, his grades suffered. Yet he eventually found balance and maintained his academic scholarship during his undergraduate years. Wayne's InterVarsity group became a second family and started to shape his thinking about priorities and friends. At the first InterVarsity retreat he attended, the speaker challenged him to let go of anything that was keeping him from full devotion to God. For Wayne, that meant breaking up with his high school sweetheart. He did not see her as being as committed to missions as he was, and he felt that she was holding him back spiritually. So while he was home for Thanksgiving, he broke off their relationship.

In the fall of Wayne's junior year, he was at a Grace Bible Church meeting and heard a freshman nurse named Sally Folger give her testimony about wanting to go on the mission field. That night, he called his mother on the phone to tell her he had met his future wife. Her name was Sally.

Wayen graduation fom the University of Michigan

Chapter 3 - Sally's Early Years:

Bernard Folger met Valdene (Val) Elitha North at a country barn dance near the town of Galesburg, Michigan soon after Val graduated from Bellevue High School. They were married September 13, 1936. Val gave Barnard the pet name "Curly", because of his curley hair, and it was soon the only way he was referred to by everyone.

Following Sally's birth came two more Folger children: a brother James, known as Jim and a sister Sandra, known as Sandi. Both Val and Curly worked factory jobs to support their young family. Curly earned his wages on the night shift for Kellogg's, and Val worked in the cafeteria at Post. The two incomes eventually allowed them to buy an old house in town on a half-acre with a wide variety of fruit trees.

Curly was an eager new home owner. He had begun cleaning up the orchard when an unexpected trial added suffering to this joyous season. Curly was trimming one of the cherry trees when a branch broke. He fell, catching his lower leg between two rungs of the ladder, breaking both bones in a compound fracture. Val was not home, so Curly sent Sally across the street to their new neighbor, Mrs. Ecklund, who called an ambulance. While the injury was devastating to Curly and had a negative impact on the family, it was Sally's first experience responding to an emergency. It also introduced her to Mrs. Ecklund, who would have a significant positive influence on her life. Mrs. Ecklund looked after the kids while Curly was at the hospital and until Val could make other arrangements.

During this time, Mrs. Ecklund introduced Sally to the Evangelical United Brethren Church. She started taking the kids to Sunday school at her church. She also introduced Val to a ladies' extension group, and, after a few years, the whole family

started going to church together. Val and Curly made friendships in the adult Sunday school class that lasted the rest of
their lives.

Another major influence on Sally's faith was Curly's mother
Edith. Some of Sally's earliest memories of talking about God
came from walking in the woods with Grandma Edith. As Edith
and Sally took walks in the forest, Edith would teach Sally the
names of the wildflowers and birds and that God made them.
Sally was special, Grandma Edith told her, because she was like
the daughter Edith never had. Sally loved to stay the night at
Grandma Edith's house. On those nights, her Grandma Edith
would read her the Bible.

A common method at the time for churches to bring the Gospel
to a community was to have evening meetings where people
could invite friends and family that were not a part of the
church to hear a special message. The family occasionally attended these evening meetings.

While she was in junior high, Sally attended one of those meetings with Val and Curly present, Sally felt called to go (to the
front of the church to make a prayerful commitment.). She recalls the internal struggle. Going forward was an emotional experience where she was overwhelmed and in tears. Sally
prayed what Evangelical churches often call "the sinner's
prayer": "Dear God, forgive me of sin and come into my heart."
As she prayed, people praying for Sally surrounded her.

Sally's life changed after this experience of accepting God's for-
giveness. She felt confident that Jesus was real and that her relationship with Him was a personal one. She began to be aware
of the presence of the Holy Spirit talking to her. She began reading the Bible daily and memorizing scripture. She also found

herself reading books from the church library. Grace Livingston Hill's novels strongly influenced her ideals about relating to men.

Not long after her conversion experience, Sally was in church when a visiting medical missionary spoke of her work in Africa. Her last slide showed a mountain. She closed saying, "Behind those mountains are people who have never heard of Christ. Someone needs to go there." Sally clearly heard a voice in her heart, "Sally, I want you to go there." She did not know where "that mountain" was, but she knew she needed to follow where God would lead her. Looking back, it appeared similar to a photo she has of the Sepik area of New Guinea.

As Sally approached the end of high school, she was faced with the decision of where to go to college. Most of her friends and family did not plan on going to college, but Sally was certain she wanted to go, and she was certain she wanted to be a nurse. This clarity was in part shaped by her commitment to going on the mission field, knowing that nursing was a great skill set to have.

She wanted to go to the Christian college. She reasoned that she would not stand out so much if those around her were also Christians. Her family and pastor all supported this approach, and the pastor started guiding Sally to the local denominational college. Sally had a Christian high school counselor who felt strongly that she should get the best nursing education possible. She encouraged Sally to look at other options. At that time, the University of Michigan nursing program was considered the best in the state. Sally had great grades and was one of the few students at her local high school who actually had a chance at acceptance to the University of Michigan. She prayed for God to show her the right school. Even though it went against her initial plan, Sally felt certain God was asking her to apply to the state university. Her pastor and family advised against the big state university, fearing that going there would cause her to lose her faith.

Then there was the issue of finances. The private school was very expensive and the nursing program at the local community college was almost free. The University of Michigan would cost something in between. She felt peace in applying to U of M.

In June, 1955, Sally had been accepted at the university and graduated from high school but she still needed a job for the summer. Here is her memory of events.

> *I remember well the Saturday just before summer jobs were to begin, and I had heard nothing from my applications. Most of the girls had found work as secretaries or clerks in stores. I was sitting in the window sill at the upstairs landing of their family home, where I often read my Bible or poetry or sang as I looked over the large back lots. 'Why didn't I get a job, Lord? How will I go to the University?' I asked. I tried to encourage myself by reading the poems in Streams in the Desert (by L.B. Cowman), trying not to face what not getting a job would mean. Reading the vivid portrayals in these poems gave me confidence and took my mind off my predicament. Suddenly the words of a poem I was reading were expressing just exactly how I felt. I read them over several times.*

> *Waiting, yes, patiently waiting*

> *Till next steps made plain shall be,*

> *To hear with an inner hearing*

The plan that Thou hast for me."

Suddenly I felt an assurance that God would let me know just what to do in time. I jumped down and ran over to my neighbor, Mrs. Ecklund, who had first started me in church. 'God is going to get me the right job so I can go to the University,' I told her. After talking with her I returned home; the telephone was ringing. The voice at the other end said, 'Can you report to work at Kellogg's cafeteria at 7:00 Monday morning?

The job was just what I had asked for: a higher paying factory job without being on the monotonous 'line'. We wore uniforms so I did not have to spend money on clothes.

Sally also enjoyed her first boyfriend that summer. They met at a Youth for Christ citywide youth meeting. Jim told her he wanted to be a missionary. They spent the summer together, and their relationship was full of passion. They were starting to talk about marriage, but as September approached he was drafted into the Navy, and she went to the University of Michigan.

Sally had not received her acceptance letter from the University of Michigan until after the scholarship deadline had passed, so a scholarship was not an option. Val and Curly offered to pay the first year, but Sally was on her own after that. She discovered she could work for meals in her dormitory cafeteria, allowing her to save enough money to pay half her tuition. Her parents then agreed to pay half the first year; and half again the second year. She was not sure where the money would come from after that.

Sally took the bus from a short summer camp to the university.

She started getting harassed by three soldiers at the station where she waited to transfer. A young man stepped in and chased off the soldiers. His name was Lloyd; he was working on his PhD at Michigan State. Lloyd was a Christian, and he and Sally hit it off and starting writing to each other. Lloyd told Sally about InterVarsity Christian Fellowship and about Grace Bible Church. Sally found the InterVarsity group and the church the first week of college.

Sally's freshman year was full: between her heavy class load and her job at the cafeteria, she did not have much free time. Sally felt so small and insignificant among the beautiful buildings at the great University. Still, her relationship with God was strong. She felt close to Him. She poured out her heart to him and asked Him to help with everything. Sally gives credit to the Lord for guiding her to get involved in both Grace Bible Church and InterVarsity.

Besides Lloyd, two other men had become a part of Sally's university life. Stan was a freshman--a quiet, understanding bookworm. He helped Sally with her English composition course and the Great Books course. They would go to church together and go out for coffee. They would talk on their walks back to the dorm. He was a good friend.

Wayne was an outgoing passionate junior and a leader in Inter-Varsity. He asked Sally out regularly. They met at InterVarsity meetings and at concerts and went out for walks in the parks. Sally loved his directness and confidence. He was passionate about his faith and was interested in the mission field. Wayne's touch caused a reaction in her that she had not experienced with the other men. It made her nervous and caused her to resist holding hands or a hug from him.

Sally was confused and torn between these relationships and

felt guilty about leading these men on. She planned to be a single missionary nurse. She began to pray for guidance. While she loved the attention, she felt the need to deepen a relationship with only one man at a time.

Sally's discomfort with so many relationships came to a head right before Christmas that year. She worked to keep them from meeting each other. Stan showed up at her dorm to help Sally's roommate prepare for final exams. He gave her a beautiful silver cross necklace. Stan was still in the dorm when Wayne came by to take her on a study date. The date had to be cut short, because Lloyd had arranged to drive her back to Battle Creek for Christmas vacation. On that trip, Lloyd gave her a red leather-covered Scofield Bible, which she kept for most of her life. It was clear from the conversation that his interest in Sally had progressed; he wanted to be more than a brother in Christ. She made an effort near the end of that ride to discourage a closer relationship.

Over Christmas she felt obligated to reciprocate their gifts. She made identical boxes of her homemade caramels, toffee, and fudge for each of the men and mailed them off.

A few nights after she arrived home and after everyone in the family had gone to bed, Jim, her boyfriend that summer came into the house. He walked into her bedroom. Sally was deeply offended. She called her brother from the next bedroom to give her support. She realized by then that Jim would not be an appropriate choice, nor was he sincere in wanting to be a missionary. She made her refusal clear that night as she sent him out of the house.

Over Christmas holiday Sally thought a lot about her need to have no more than one boyfriend and returned to school in January seeking advice from her friends. Her roommates liked

Stan, he was cuter and kinder to them. Sally did feel more relaxed with Stan. Their conversations were more about class topics. He patiently helped her understand difficult concepts. Stan had already let her know indirectly that he really liked her. Of course, they were only freshmen and couldn't get too serious anyway. So she decided to follow their advice and was preparing to tell Wayne she was not interested.

Sally looked for an opportunity to broach the subject with Wayne, but she found their conversations interesting and did not want to give those up. Wayne was the missionary chairman for their InterVarsity group that year and invited Sally to work with him on a mission promotion strategy for the local InterVarsity chapter. Wayne and Sally talked for hours about the mission needs.

Sally found Wayne's passion about doing missions better exciting and appealing. For example, Wayne was frustrated that the prevailing relationship between missionaries and the local people was colonial and condescending, like a parent and a child. He viewed this paternalism as wrong and ineffective, and was convinced there was a better way. Wayne and Sally discussed the concept of a tribal-run church. He was excited about all he heard about the Baliem Valley opening up in Papua. These types of regular conversation made Sally reluctant to have a conversation that would damage the relationship.

Finally, Sally got up enough nerve to face the unpleasant conversation. She recalls the evening going like this:

I did enjoy talking with Wayne. I dreaded having to say anything, but it was terribly unfair to lead him on. I finally plunged in. "I don't feel we should see each other anymore."

He winced as the smile left his face. I hedged and tried to give some reasons, but nothing changed his mood. Finally, he said, "Let's go outside." We went to an isolated stairway outside the dorm. It had gotten very cold. I began to shiver, but kept my distance. "I really have enjoyed being with you. I...I thought you liked being with me," he said. It was the first time I had seen him at a loss for words and confused.

I tried to explain that I wasn't unhappy with him, but what I said didn't sound reasonable even to me. Somehow, I gave him the impression I didn't trust him. I had hoped to hide that. "Anyway, it's too confusing going with both you and Stan. I think I'll go with Stan for a while." It wasn't the way I had wanted to say it, but........

He looked at the ground, putting his hands into his pockets. He reminded me of a beaten puppy. I felt a strong desire to reach out and comfort him, but I didn't dare touch him, not after my experiences with Jim. "I don't want to be fooled by my emotions again," I thought.

Finally, he spoke slowly and rather desperately. "Sally, I know it's too soon to ask you this. I don't expect you to answer me now. But......I love you. I had hoped you might consider being my wife someday."

I gasped, unable to hide my surprise. I wondered if I heard rightly and how I could answer and not hurt him anymore. I had wanted to keep him from caring too much, but it was already too late. I said, "I'm sorry, Wayne. I........ I didn't know you cared so much. Forget what I said. I.... I'll think about it."

Then I realized that I really cared too. Bewildered, I quickly excused myself.

Following this conversation, and contrary to her original goal, Sally broadened her involvement with Wayne. She went home to visit his family. His family history of mission work and his uncle's role in starting New Tribes Mission intrigued her. The fact that his father worked full-time and preached on Sundays also impressed her.

A change in their relationship occurred in February. Wayne and Sally went with a married couple to Pontiac, Michigan to listen to a presentation given by the widows of the five missionaries martyred among the Aucas in Ecuador a few months earlier. The church was showing a film strip of the attempts to witness to Aucas and was interviewing the widows. Wayne and Sally rode home from that meeting in the back seat. He gently brought her close, and they kissed. She was overwhelmed by the sense of closeness. This kiss began a very physically intense season in their relationship. The intensity scared them both, and they did not want to dishonor each other or God in the ways they related to each other physically. They also did not want to make a life-changing decision based solely on their physical passion for each other.

In mid-March an InterVarsity speaker challenged the couples in the group to test the strength of their relationships by staying away from each other for a month. Based on this recommendation, Wayne and Sally decided to break up and separate from each other for a while to see where things went.

Sally was not happy during the break-up and began to pray earnestly for guidance. One day, she went to a small prayer chapel in a church bordering the university campus. She skipped all her classes and meals and spent the entire day in prayer and reading Scripture. That evening, she felt God's assurance and made a decision to get back together with Wayne. Over the next two months, they discussed many life issues. In June, they were on the way back to her dorm from the Sunday morning church service. Wayne tried to make his burning question sound casual, afraid of being refused. "I wonder where we will be five years from now," he remarked.

"I think we will be married," Sally answered.

"I would like that," Wayne replied. The exchange opened into a conversation about their future together, and the two began to seriously consider marriage.

Shortly after this conversation, Wayne's summer job as a surveyor took him to Alaska, hindering his communication with Sally. Their letters took six weeks to get a reply back.

Wayne's high salary evaporated in living and travel expense, and he came home with nothing but great experiences and a few gifts. Hoping to save money on the return trip east so he could buy Sally a ring, Wayne tried to hitchhike from Seattle. Instead, the driver was going south to Red Bluff where his Uncle Wayne lived, and Wayne took the opportunity to see him. That visit in California took longer than expected. In order to get back to the University of Michigan in time for class he had to use his money for plane fare instead. The summer had not played out the way either of them hoped, but they were still very much in love and intent on marriage. Sally never did get an engagement ring.

Chapter 4 - Wayne and Sally Together

Wayne was elected president of the local InterVarsity chapter for the academic year following his summer in Alaska. The couple decided to keep their engagement secret, because they did not want the relationship to interfere with the ministry. Even Wayne's closest friends did not realize how serious his relationship with Sally had become.

That fall, both Wayne and Sally jumped into missions and evangelism in dramatic ways. They were committed to each other and committed to missions. Any energy they had left after meeting their school and work responsibilities went into learning what they could about mission work.

The InterVarsity group invited Dr. John Stott of England that fall with a ministry team joining with the group's local executive team. This program expanded Wayne and Sally's vision for missions, giving them new respect for other Christian denominations' mission programs. Wayne and Sally read broadly about all aspects of mission work. They spent hours together discussing and evaluating current missionary practices and the advantages of the indigenous church. They wanted to bring the Gospel, the good news of Jesus, to remote places without stifling the native cultures. There were too many stories of colonial missionaries forcing the villages to change in very unhealthy ways. Many of the ideas that shaped Wayne and Sally's work on cross-cultural missiology were born out of the research they did in this time period.

Wayne had decided when he was very young that there had to be a better way to reach remote cultures than the martyr path his uncles had taken. He was also convinced that the colonial mission approach was not right. This need to develop a better way to reach remote cultures for the gospel began to be a driving passion in his life and Sally's as well.

On the personal relationship side, they avoided being alone together and developed boundaries when it came to their physical relationship. By November they decided it was silly to stay apart until June, so they set their wedding date for January 26, 1957. Part of their reasoning was that by getting married, Wayne would reduce the risk of getting drafted in the Korean War, since married men were lower on the draft priority than single men. They picked winter break because they wanted time for a short honeymoon before school started again. Wayne's friends were shocked when they announced their upcoming wedding. The InterVarsity group leadership tried to convince Wayne and Sally to wait until summer, but in the end they supported the couple's decision to marry in January. After the wedding announcement, Wayne and Sally arranged for Edith and Marion to meet Val and Curly.

Sally and Val used a fictitious wedding plan Sally had developed to marry "Prince Charming" in a 12th grade marriage and family class for the wedding. Val finalized the wedding plans and financed the event, consulting Sally over the phone on color choices and other details. Edith found a beautiful wedding dress. The family pitched in to make the bridesmaid dresses. It was a small wedding in Sally's church in Battle Creek. Wayne's father, Marion, officiated the ceremony.

Wedding formal January 26, 1957. Left to right - Curly, Val, Sally, Wayne, Edith, Marion

Sally's maid of honor was Jan Titsworth, a friend of Wayne's before Sally came on the scene. Jan had since become one of Sally's closest friends at the University. The other bridesmaids were Sally's aunt Joan and her sister Sandy. Sally's much younger sister Sherry was the flower girl. Wayne's brother Doug was his best man. Sally's brother Jim and Wayne's brother Gordon were ushers. It was a lovely cake and punch wedding with mints and nuts at the reception held at the church reception hall. Two carloads of InterVarsity friends came from the University of Michigan.

After the wedding, Wayne and Sally spent their first night near Lansing, then went to a motel in Grayling in northern Michigan. They went snow skiing, tobogganing, and took long walks together in the snow-covered forests and fields.

Following their honeymoon Wayne and Sally settled into a studio apartment near campus. Bicycles were their only transportation, and they found themselves riding miles up and down hills daily. Engrossed in their physical relationship, they did not study much in the evenings. As a result, their grades suffered. Sally finished the semester with a passing grade in Biochemistry, but the semester's outcomes made her realize that school needed to be a higher priority.

Wayne and Sally's parents decided that since the two were now married, Wayne and Sally were financially on their own. The semester was financially tight. They relied entirely on Wayne's part-time drafting job and some scholarship aid from the Grace Bible Church Scholarship fund.

After Wayne's graduation in June 1957, they moved into a studio apartment in a house near the hospital where Sally was a student nurse. It had a separate kitchenette but they shared a bathroom with the elderly owners. Wayne got a full-time construction job and bought a used car on credit with four monthly payments.

That fall Sally struggled with a deep sense of failure. She had always done well at school and worked even harder to keep up her grades. Many of Sally's friends had dropped out after their first year, but Sally struggled on through the rigorous program. Sally's fear of pregnancy caused a hesitancy in the bedroom that impacted their relationship.

She became more aware of her personal weaknesses, but she found it difficult to face them. She also became more aware of Wayne's weaknesses. He was questioning her more "naïve" faith. His arguments seemed convincing to Sally, and this strained their relationship. They began to question each other's commitment to the marriage. Sally's stress showed in anger.

Wayne pulled away emotionally. Wayne's little brother Gordon was drifting from his Christian faith, and Wayne spent a lot of weekends in Detroit trying to reason with him.

Sally looked to Scripture and found verses to calm her fears. She heard God say in Hebrews, "I will never leave you nor forsake you." And, in Philippians, she read, "He which has begun a good work in you will perform it till the day of Jesus Christ......and He will keep your heart and mind in Christ Jesus." Sally meditated on these verses, and they helped restore a measure of confidence in God and some relief in the depression.

Wayne was patient in Sally's low point. He assured her that he would not leave her even when he was angry. This created a new trust and closeness in their relationship. Sally began to confide in him about how she was thinking and feeling, the same way she used to with God.

As they approached their first anniversary, they began to talk openly about the idea that they should never have married. Sally had hoped a good start in marriage would help them "live happily ever after." But things were not so simple. They resigned themselves to that fact that divorce was sin (wrong in the eyes of God as they understood it from their upbringing and from their reading of the Bible), and they reasoned that even if the marriage had not been in God's will in the beginning, it was now. Wayne tried to reaffirm his love for Sally by planning a beautiful anniversary meal at an expensive local hotel and restaurant named the Dearborn Inn, but that did not bring back the joy in their relationship.

One day, in a moment of anger, Sally packed her stuff and prepared to leave. Wayne stayed calm and tried to reason with her. This low point in their marriage became a turning point. Sally turned to God for help with her conflicts. She read Jesus' teachings about divorce in Matthew 19:5-9 KJV. Key points impacted her: "... for this cause shall a man leave father and mother, and shall cleave to his wife: they twain shall be one flesh. Wherefore they are no more twain, but one flesh. What therefore God hath joined together, let not man put asunder.... Whosoever shall put away his wife, except it be for fornication, and shall marry another, committeth adultery,"

She discussed the passage with Wayne. Then it dawned on them: "We cannot break this marriage," they decided. "We pledged, 'Till death do us part.'" They looked back on this discussion several years later and concluded—"that was the real beginning of our marriage." Since they were going to be married for life, they would be best off working harder on their relationship. They accepted what their pastor had told them before the marriage, "You cannot each go halfway in the relationship, because neither knows where the line is. Both have to go all the way, but it will feel like the other hasn't gone much more than half." They determined to find ways to work through the strains in their relationship. In the spring, they moved to a better living situation: an attractive one-bedroom apartment that afforded them more privacy. It was next to a park but required a two mile bike ride to the hospital.

Meanwhile, for Wayne, the change from passion to disillusionment in their marriage became one of the experiences that set him on a new journey of introspection and questioning. Where the two of them had felt so confident in hearing the voice of God before, now there was doubt.

Another experience contributed to Wayne's questioning that spring. Wayne and Sally attended an overcrowded Oral Roberts healing service. The only seats that remained were side front, in full view of the sound control panel. They witnessed sound manipulation and inappropriate coaching of some of the people who believed they were healed of deafness. That incident created further doubt. Wayne was beginning to agree with many of the Christian intellectuals at University of Michigan who believed that, while God was real, He was not involved in our daily lives.

The risk of the draft was still real; the United States needed a large standing army to keep the U.S.S.R. from expanding its territory under Stalin's leadership. Wayne received a card in the mail requiring him to update his draft information and placing him on notice that he was now eligible for the draft. On the bottom of the card, an underlined sentence said that the draft would be deferred for students enrolled in qualified universities. Wayne began to consider continuing his education. Going back to school could keep him from getting drafted and spending years in an army far from where Sally was studying. This was a big decision, and so Wayne sought the advice of Professor Kenneth Pike at the University of Michigan. Dr. Pike was a Wycliffe leader and one of Wayne's mentors. Wayne had taken his beginning linguistics course at the university, and Dr. Pike was the college student Sunday school teacher at their church.

Dr. Pike thought Christian missionaries needed to grow in their understanding of anthropology in order to be better equipped to bring the Gospel to remote cultures. He had progressive ideas about church growth and a local community's ability to provide their own leadership. But he recognized the issue was complicated and that he did not have all the answers. He wanted more Christians to study at a higher level to help work through the issues with more training. Dr. Pike encouraged Wayne to go back to school and get his master's degree in anthropology and avoid the draft. Wayne went with the advice.

Unlike the engineering department, the anthropology department was openly atheistic. They demanded students answer questions with the department's worldview in mind. If a student disagreed with the professor he or she was allowed to write at the top of the paper the following statement:

"All questions are answered in accordance with the ideas taught by this course." A sample question might be: *True or false. Man created god in his own image.* The answer that would be marked "correct" was "True."

Wayne was already struggling with his own doubts, and this openly atheistic context continued to push him away from the idea that God was actively involved in the world. Wayne started to buy into the idea that religion could be a fabrication of the human mind. He had seen Christians interpreting as miracles events that he judged as simply coincidence. Wayne feared he might be a victim of it himself. He spent months trying to make rational arguments for the Christian faith as opposed to culture determining what people believed.

Sally argued that God is more involved with us than we think, but Wayne was not quick to resolve his inner struggle. She resorted to praying while Wayne returned to his friend and mentor. Dr. Pike challenged Wayne to always look at the basic assumptions behind a theory. If one assumes there is no supernatural, the logical conclusion of rational thinking will be that there is no God. On the other hand, if one assumes God as creator and seeker of individual people, then the equally logical conclusion will be that biblical teaching is true. Pike reasoned that the logic was tied to the assumptions--make a different assumption and you reach different conclusions. Both sides had good logic, but embraced different basic assumptions as the foundation for their logic. Dr. Pike challenged Wayne to consider the outcome of each paradigm before embracing one worldview or the other.

Wayne came out of that conversation believing both paradigms were possible. He began to think about people and evidence of lives lived under each paradigm. While he could explain away some of the miraculous healings he had witnessed, he could not explain away the transformed lives. He had seen so many people's lives radically changed through the church. He had watched families brought back together and people go from defeated by hardships to victorious over them. Wayne compared those outcomes to the atheists he knew. They were, for the most part, self-centered and bitter, and tended to be sarcastic and cynical. His memories of the good that he had witnessed in Jesus' name began to give him comfort. Even if it might be all self-deception, it was a good deception and he could help others with it. He embraced the idea that a life of serving others philanthropically was better than living for oneself.

This conclusion led to another struggle. Was foreign missions the most productive way to serve humanity? Many of the missionaries Wayne met seemed eager to bring their ideas to "the third world." After all, the US was progressive, some reasoned. Our ideas would improve the world. We were the richest most powerful country in the world, the thinking went. *Of course, our ideas are best.* Wayne and Sally were both very wary of this type of colonial thinking. If they were going to bring the Gospel to remote tribes, they wanted to do it in a way that would really benefit the community through transformed lives.

Chapter 5 – Preparing for Missions

By this time, Sally was in her last term of nursing school, and they decided to continue on the path towards the mission field. Wayne was not finished with his master's degree, but he wanted more answers from a Christian worldview. Most mission boards were requiring a year of Bible training. After Sally graduated in June of 1959, she worked at the hospital over the summer. In the fall of that year, they headed off to Columbia Bible College.

One thing that really impressed them about the professors at Columbia was the love they saw in action. Wayne was again reminded of the transforming power of the Christian Faith in the life of true believers. This was in stark contrast to the leadership of the Anthropology Department at University of Michigan. He was not always impressed with the logic of the Bible college professors' answers to his questions, but he was encouraged by the way they helped others. The redeeming power of the Gospel to bring people out of a self-destructive lifestyle was hard for his logical brain to ignore.

With her bachelor of science degree in nursing behind her and her husband back from the brink of atheism, Sally began to relax and enjoy life again. She was pregnant, and when Edith Lynne was born in December of 1959, she dropped out of Columbia to stay home with the baby. She had more free time than she had had in years, and she used it to study Scripture and read books on missions and faith.

As mission committee chair for InterVarsity, Wayne had worked with a lot of mission organizations. During their time at Columbia, they wrestled with which mission organization to join. They liked Ken Pike; they liked Wycliffe's goals of Bible translation; they liked their emphasis on letting the people read God's Word in their own language to find the answers to life's problems. Wayne and Sally became friends with Wycliffe couples, including Lyle and Helen Scholz and Jim and Dorothy Wheatley, who convinced them to take a summer course at the Summer Institute of Linguistics in Norman, Oklahoma.

Sally's youngest sister Sherry came to Oklahoma with them and helped dress Edie, take her to the nursery, and entertain her in the evenings while Wayne and Sally were studying. The skill-oriented courses were intense, but the many stories of what God was doing around the world convinced them this was what God had called them to do. One of the most stimulating experiences was hearing Cameron Townsend, Wycliffe's founder, teach his unforgettable theme song, written by Charles Wesley:

"Faith, mighty faith, the promise sees,

And looks to God alone;

Laughs at impossibilities,

And shouts, 'It shall be done!'"

They would desperately need the encouragement of this chorus over the next few years. During that summer of 1960 in Oklahoma, they applied and were accepted to Wycliffe Bible Translators. The next step was the required three-month jungle training camp in Chiapas, Mexico.

Wayne had quit his engineering job when they went to Oklahoma and their savings account was running low. They wrote their first prayer letter in October of 1960 just before leaving for the jungle training camp. They were already thinking about serving in New Guinea by then. They mentioned eastern New Guinea having over five hundred languages without God's

Word; that was the part of the island where Wycliffe was working. They visited churches, asking for prayer and financial support, but still they did not have enough money for Jungle Camp. Finally, they sold their canoe, but still they did not have enough money. Wayne called Wycliffe and told them they did not have the funds to go to camp. "I guess we cannot go," he said.

Wayne and Sally argued. Sally believed they were meant to go and wanted to continue praying. Yet Wayne was still struggling with the idea that God was interested and involved in their personal lives. Nevertheless, they prayed and asked God for the money to go. That afternoon they got a call from their Ann Arbor church. A student had donated two hundred dollars for the trip. This was the first in a series of lessons that Wayne would learn about depending on a God who was actively involved in their lives.

Wayne and Sally loved camping. Jungle Camp was camping with a purpose. They learned many practical things, including how to deal with tropical disease, and how to build and live in shelters from jungle materials, how to make clay cooking stoves, and how to repair pressure lamps and small motors. But this was also their first exposure to tribal culture. The camp was near the lands of the Tzeltal Indian Tribe, which had a thriving indigenous church. This experience began to solidify Wayne and Sally's commitment to an indigenous church approach to missions. Wayne wrote this in his letter to their supporting churches:

"There are many congregations of believers here who were won to Christ by fellow Indians. These in turn are sending out lay evangelists to other villages. There is no need for more foreign missionaries to the Tzeltals."

The second half of the Wycliffe training camp was the wilderness survival. They told Sally she could not stay to participate in it, because she was pregnant with their second child, Joy, and would be too far from a doctor's care. So, she and Edie flew back to Michigan and spent the rest of the time in Battle Creek with her parents while Wayne stayed on by himself.

Wayne was doing his devotions one morning and read the passage where John the Baptist is talking about Christ to his disciples. John the Baptist says, "I must decrease, but He must increase". The message jumped out of the page at Wayne, and he was sure it was God speaking directly to him. Hearing God's voice so directly was a new experience for Wayne. This began a new phase in his spiritual journey.

Wayne in Jungle Camp

Wayne also wrote home about having to be rescued by fellow campers because he built his shelter too close to the river. As a civil engineer, that hurt his pride, and he realized God was helping him make the needed changes in his attitude. The camp wanted him to stay a little longer and help with some survey work. He wanted to go back to Battle Creek so he would not miss the baby's birth. Wayne believed God was asking him to stay there and do the work and trust that he would be back in time. Not wanting to miss his daughter's birth, he ignored the voice telling him to stay and returned to Battle Creek before the work was completed. Later, through a series of circumstances that ended with a blizzard, Wayne missed Joy's birth. Wayne took this as confirmation that the in-

L-R Sally, Curly, Grandma Edith, Edie

ner voice had been God and that he should have finished the job in Mexico.

It is clear in the tone of Wayne's letters that his doubts about the reality of God's existence were gone, and he was now struggling to understand God's active presence in his personal life. His years of university training made it difficult for him to embrace "blind faith". His experience exploring the idea that God is a fabrication of man had changed his understanding and thought process, causing him to be very careful and selective about what he chose to believe. This internal conversation was the beginnings of Wayne's study of the impact worldview plays in a person's belief system.

They were scheduled to go back to Oklahoma to take essential Wycliffe courses. The day before they were to leave for Oklahoma, they borrowed Sally's brother Jim's boat for a relaxing

Sunday afternoon on a small lake near Battle Creek without the children. When they approached the narrow neck of the hourglass shaped lake, two drunk men decided to turn their boat around without looking, ramming into Wayne and Sally's boat. The drunken men's boat struck Wayne's right chest as his arm was raised in turning away, knocking both him and Sally unconscious. The drunken boat driver and his friend were thrown from their boat. The now driverless boat spun back around and ran over Wayne's boat a second time.

A lifeguard on the beach nearby observed the accident and called the ambulance. He jumped in his life boat and towed Wayne and Sally's boat to shore where the ambulance was already waiting. Sally was conscious before the ambulance arrived, but Wayne was only vaguely aware that he was being placed in an ambulance.

Sally was bruised, her pelvis was damaged, some teeth were broken, but she had no life-threatening injuries. She was treated in the emergency room, then could go home. Wayne was in critical condition. His ribcage had over fifteen fractures to five ribs; his lung was punctured and had collapsed. His scapula and pelvis were also broken.

He was stabilized in the ER and transferred to the intensive care unit. His parents were notified and made the three-hour drive from Detroit. Sally stayed with him as family came and went. His condition slowly worsened. He became weaker and weaker. By the third day he had stopped breathing several times. The standard chest tubes and suction to clear the lung cavity were not working. He was drowning in his own fluids, and the doctors could not figure out how to remove the fluid.

Sally called their supporting churches to pray that Wednesday afternoon. That evening, while several churches were praying the doctor came in and ushered Sally from the room. She went to the hospital chapel with Wayne's mother to pray. Sally sat in the chapel sobbing uncontrollably until she was completely exhausted. She begged God not to take Wayne. He had grown to mean more to Sally than her faith. In a moment of utter despair, she sensed that she needed to give her husband up. She felt a gentle voice asking her to give him over.

"Give him to me please, Sally," God asked her tenderly.

She screamed and cried, "No! I can't... I can't. I can't!" Then as exhaustion overtook her, she prayed, "Oh God, you can have him. Let Your will be done." Immediately, she felt a sense of relief and peace, and she stopped crying.

At the same time as Sally was giving Wayne up to God and churches were praying, a doctor was in the ICU doing what he could to save Wayne. The practice of drawing fluid directly from the lung cavity was not common in 1961, but this doctor had heard of its effectiveness. He stuck a large needle through Wayne's back into the area of lung cavity that had collapsed and drew out a lot of blood. This immediately restored Wayne's breathing and started him on the road to recovery. For Sally and the family, the time, the prayer, and the circumstances surrounding Wayne's survival were confirmation of God's healing hand. This event increased Sally's faith and strengthened her resolve to trust God.

Wayne stayed a month in intensive care on a special circular turning frame. Sally applied for a job in the same hospital, working days. The family pitched in to help care for Edie and Joy to make that possible. Val worked evening shift, and took responsibility for the children in the morning. Sally's sister Sandy worked the night shift and watched the girls in the afternoon. Sally's youngest sister Sherry also helped take care of

Edie and Joy. Sally took them evenings and through the night. Between the four of them they looked after the babies. In July, Wayne came home. The rest of the summer he slowly recovered in Val and Curly's home. He helped some when he was strong enough.

The girls were not easy and Joy struggled with colic. It finally stopped when she was switched to whole milk, but it was a long four months and everyone was exhausted.

Wayne in a rotating traction bed

By the end of the summer, Wayne felt strong enough to face the world again. They would not get their Wycliffe field assignment until they had completed that second linguistics course, but it would not be offered again until the following summer. Wayne was too weak to return to his construction inspection job, but he did want to finish his Anthropology Degree at the University of Michigan.

They moved back to Ann Arbor in late August where Wayne found a part-time drafting job, while Sally worked the evening shift at the hospital. They hired a babysitter to cover the evening gap in schedule when neither of them were available to watch Joy and Edie. Wayne would work in the morning, school in the afternoon, and then stay home and take care of the kids in the evening. Wayne was not much of a cook so Sally would prepare the meals before she left for work in the afternoon. Then he would heat up what she had prepared. Sally was scheduled home at 1 am, but often did not actually finish up until 2 or 3 am.

The girls were up way before she had enough sleep. Meeting their needs became overwhelming. Joy was struggling with inner ear infections; she would scream in pain. Sally spent a lot of time taking her to doctors. Wayne and Sally felt trapped. They did not want to share how difficult life was or their struggles with the church staff, because they needed their support when they went on the mission field. Wayne tried to reach out to his mother and tell her how tough things were getting with Sally, but Edith shut him down and would not let him speak ill of Sally. Sally knew she was beyond her limit and needed something to change. Their schedule was just not sustainable, but they were not sure what to do about it. Sally was filled with self-doubt and guilt, and she turned to singing, and praying. She begged God for supernatural ability to be the loving mom she knew she needed to be. As she rocked the kids she would sing of her love to them.

One night, she woke up overwhelmed with a sense of God's presence. She was filled with praise and gathered the girls around her, and they sang every praise and worship song they could think of. This event gave Sally strength and encouragement. Being reminded that God was there and on her side helped her face the struggles of that season.

In January, Wayne received an academic scholarship which allowed him to work fewer hours and be home more. They stumbled along. Wayne's program had changed so profoundly during the two years he had been away that he was put at a significant disadvantage. There had been a paradigm shift in the way scholars perceived and talked about Archaeology. No one warned him that there had been such a change. The questions on that part of the comprehensive M.A. exam were similar to what had been asked in previous years, but the correct answers were entirely different. He failed that part and did not obtain a master's degree in anthropology. He was devastated. All that striving and sacrifice, the crazy schedule and the sleepless nights, and he would have to give it up or try again later.

About that same time, they discovered that Sally was pregnant again. They were careful with protection, but they were apparently a very fertile couple. This was not a baby they needed in this season of their lives. The news was a blow at an already low point. The semester was over. It was time to return to Oklahoma and finish the linguistics course they needed to get their field assignment. They packed up the car with a comfortable area for the girls and headed to Norman, Oklahoma.

They were traveling through Rockford, Illinois, when Sally experienced severe back pain. The doctor at Rockford Hospital discovered a partially ruptured disk that was pinching nerves in her spinal column. Wayne's special cousin Rosemary and her husband lived nearby. They welcomed Wayne and the girls while Sally remained in the hospital in pelvic traction for four days. She was released with pain relievers. She was given a traction belt with weights to relieve the pressure on the spinal column and strict instructions to stay in bed with the traction belt 23 hours per day.

What a shock to their plans to go for the required linguistic courses. Wayne and Sally were afraid to cancel again. They did not want to delay the mission field one more year and feared what the mission board would do. The timing was almost identical to the last accident they had—just as they were leaving for training. They wondered about the possibility that this was a spiritual attack trying to keep them from the mission field. They discussed it, prayed and asked family for help and guidance.

Wayne had a fifteen-year-old cousin named Merrilee Shailor who agreed to fly to Norman and help look after Edie and Joy so Wayne could take the essential courses. They had two rooms with bunk beds in the large dormitory. Merrilee and the girls in one; Wayne and Sally in the other. Wayne set up the traction on the end of the lower bunk for Sally. She was determined to follow the doctor's orders to stay in traction in bed essentially 23 hours and went to class for the core course she needed while up one hour. A local Cheyenne Indian woman would come to Sally's bed side and help her with the tribal linguistics portion of the course.

Merrilee helped dress the girls and took them to the day care provided. She and Wayne picked up the girls and took them to the dining room to eat. Some who did not know Wayne thought he had a very young wife. After the meal, Wayne brought Sally her meals in bed. Merrilee was also able to join in some of the teen activities.

During their time in Oklahoma, they continued to try and understand where on the mission field they should go. After much prayer and discussion, both Wayne and Sally believed they were supposed to go to New Guinea. They asked for that assignment. Later that summer Dr. Pike called Wayne up to tell him the bad news. Wycliffe did not believe they were ready for a field assignment to New Guinea with Sally's back injury. The country was too rugged. They both struggled to accept the news. Wayne resigned himself; Sally was not at peace.

Carol McKinney, Sally's Wycliffe friend from University of Michigan was teaching one of the courses. She stopped by Sally's room to encourage her. She said that God had asked her to visit Sally instead of doing her normal devotions that morning. Sally was overwhelmed by the gesture of thoughtfulness and burst into tears. Her friend starting reading from the book of Psalms:

One passage stood out--Psalms 37:34 "Wait on the Lord, and keep his way, and he shall exalt thee to inherit the land." Sally felt a strong sense of God's promise in those words. God would get them to New Guinea. She did not know when or how, but she was now confident. Wayne was not so sure and warned her about taking scripture out of context. They asked for wisdom and guidance from friends and family. Twenty friends and family members pledged to provide daily prayer for them.

Wayne and Sally returned to Detroit where Wayne had found a construction inspection job. Money was a big concern. They owed Sally's parents, her brother Jim for repairs on his boat, and hospital bills. They had no insurance coverage for the boat as a recreational vehicle. Rent in Detroit was high, but they found a reasonably priced first floor house with two bedrooms, and use of the basement and garage. The Christian lady who owned the house lived upstairs. The low price of rent helped defray expenses; the owner was very kind and sympathetic to the family.

A big reason they were in debt was the medical bills related to the boat accident. Many of Wayne and Sally's friends encouraged them to go after the drunk boat driver for the funds. The State of Michigan had ticketed the driver for reckless boating, but his lawyer was doing a very good job of keeping the money for Wayne's medical cost and the repair of Jim's boat in the driver's pocket. Wayne and Sally would have to sue the driver for the hospital bills and lawyer fees. Wayne and Sally wrestled with the idea of suing the driver. They wanted to do what was right. They were torn between the passages in the Bible about not suing people and getting free of debt so they could go to the mission field. Friends spoke on both sides. A Christian lawyer friend of Wayne's aunt offered to take their case pro bono. They felt at peace with that and went ahead with filing a lawsuit.

Grace, their landlady, encouraged them to attend Strathmoor-Judson Baptist Church with her. They liked the pastor and made many friends who took genuine interest in their plans to be Bible translators. Sally was now allowed up most of the day but was still hindered by her back and her pregnancy. She did her best to manage the house and the two girls. This was actually a good time for Sally, as she had time to enjoy the girls and read and study. She had felt completely defeated the year before and needed a change.

One of the books she read was called "The Saving Life of Christ" by Ian Thomas. Ian had jumped into service with intensity and tried to do ministry on his own strength. The book describes a transformation that involved realizing his own lack of ability and asking God for help each day. That resulted in a transformation of his experience. Wayne and Sally had heard God's voice and seen him come through in specific discreet ways, but they had not experienced victory in the way that Ian described it. The possibility of a different experience with God brought hope to Sally and she pressed Wayne to read the book.

Wayne was still very stressed out. His work was tough and the hospital debt was weighing heavy on his mind. He viewed the debt as one of many things keeping them from the mission field, but he did not have another plan. A noted section from the book caught Wayne's attention. Ian cited 1 Peter 3: 1. "They will be won over to believe by your conduct. It will not be necessary for you to say a word." This was not consistent with Sally or Wayne's experience.

Sally started a journey of prayer trying to learn to approach her walk with God differently. As she prayed, she felt new hope and new strength. She found she had renewed energy to do house work and felt the changes working. Wayne noticed and read the book also but kept that fact from her. As she prayed and trusted God, she saw more changes happen.

The lawsuit settled right before Christmas for enough money to pay off the medical bills. Wayne and Sally felt that settling for more than the amount owed would be a bad witness. The settlement cleared the way for them to request a field assignment. Thomas Wayne, "Tom" was born January 29, 1963, and was a very easy baby. Now it was just Wayne and Sally's health that were keeping them from the mission field.

By February, the debts were all paid; they had saved the $1,400 needed for the ship. They had tentatively identified the ship's departure date. Their February prayer letter reflects a subtle change in their view of God and their approach to ministry. One sentence stands out: "We long to go to New Guinea, yet we don't want to get ahead of Him." Wayne and Sally were learning to balance personal initiative with a dependency on God's guidance.

They began to pray for complete healing so they could leave for the mission field. One day Sally saw Joy heading for the street and ran out to bring her back. She stepped off the high end of the porch and wrenched her back—into place. The doctor checked it and gave his approval. Around the same time Wayne's doctor gave him a letter that stated his lungs were healed enough to travel. He told him verbally that he should not go to tropical places because the moist air might open him to tuberculosis. Formally, the doctor's note was enough for Wycliffe to give them a green light to go to New Guinea.

There was not much time between February and August to get everything ready to have all the clothes and household items they would need to live there for five years. Money was tight so Wayne continued to work full time. They visited churches on Sundays hoping to raise the supporting partners they needed. Sally struggled to keep ahead of the three children as they collected the things they would need. The standard shipping technique of the time was to pack everything in fifty-five-gallon oil barrels for shipping to the field. They ended up with thirteen barrels and a large crate.

Chapter 6 – Where are the Babies?

While Wayne and Sally were striving to make it to the mission field, Yafei and the people of Wagu village were coping with their own frustrations and disappointments. Through Yafei's recruiting efforts the village was growing. Many of the people were coming for the exposure to Western technology and food. But there was a huge problem across the region with unexplained deaths, and the Genesowayagu people were not alone in experiencing dwindling numbers.

Village shot gun. Left to right - Kwniyfo, Begai, Kiawi

There was an enterprising Chinese merchant named Chileong (pronounced chili-own) who would travel up and down the Sepik River trading tools, food, and clothing for crocodile skins, artifacts, and smoked fish.

Note: There was a story told about Chileong that during the War with Japan he cut his ship in half and sank it somewhere along the Sepik River, then lived out the war with his PNG wife's family. After the war he rebuilt it. At the time this book was written that story had not been verified.

Thanks to Chileong's trading boat, the Wagu people had a shot gun, bush knives, pots, matches, and fishing gear. For the men life was getting easier and food was much more plentiful. They were at a time of relative peace. Canoes were much easier to carve with steel axes than with stone tools. The people of Wagu were making almost enough canoes for each family to have one. Yafei was hopeful that these new Western tools would help his village thrive again.

While the men's job of hunting, building, and protecting was easier, the women were not getting the same help. They provided food and clothing for their families with what could be obtained in the forest. This included the string bags in which

they carried infants and toddlers along with everything needed for an infant to sleep and keep clean. They took full responsibility for the infants and were blamed for any illness that came upon anyone in the village.

Wagu woman bringing home the groceries

There were social expectations about what could be eaten as they worked in the jungle and what should be taken home to share. After cooking the food, the women placed each person's share on a shelf wrapped in leaves, bark or a bowl. They cut and hauled firewood. They cleaned and then cooked the game that was brought home from the hunt. They also swept the house and

Women working together carving the sago from the trunk of the tree with stone axes

yard fed dogs and other tamed animals like pigs, possums, cassowaries, wallabies, etc.

One of the more challenging and physically demanding of the Wagu's routine chores was harvesting sago. Sago Palms grow naturally in the swampy areas of the Sepik floodplain. As a primary source of calories, sago became their staple diet. One Sago Palm tree can produce 800 pounds of starch, but takes 10 to 15 years to mature into a forty-foot tall tree 18" in diameter. The tree must be cut down and harvested at the right stage in its maturity or all the work is wasted. If it is cut before starting to bud at the top of the tree, there is no starch. After blossoming, the developing seeds use up all the starch and kill the tree. Missing the harvest window remains a common issue among the Sepik peoples. After a palm was harvested, Wagus planted a small shoot nearby, but not closer to the village.

The other difficulty about sago harvesting was the location. The

71

tree roots needed to stay mostly wet and were typically located in muddy swamps full of snakes, leeches, mosquitoes, and every form of discomfort you can imagine. Each tree was completely covered with six-inch-long (10 cm) needle like thorns. The men cut the palm down and then broke the trunk up into several sections. They then split off the outer bark to gain access to the soft inner pulp.The women then took over and crushed the pulp with their stone hammers. Then the women created a washing and drainage system from key parts of the tree: a washing trough from a wide lower branch to wash the starch out of the crushed pulp; a bark fabric mesh from the top of the tree was fastened in the trough to allow suspended starch and water through. The flexible "bark" basins to collect the product were made by folding and tying the palm sheath, also from the top of the tree. The heavy starch would settle at the bottom of the bowl. They poured out the water and the sago starch would be left. Then at the end of the long day of washing the women hauled the dripping sago in string bags hung from their heads. Wet balls of sago could weigh over twenty pounds each. One woman might carry two or three at a time.

The starch ball was then dried and used to produce patties or gelatin depending on the desired meal. The sago and other food was kept in the houses wrapped in bark, and hung high in the rafter above the fire. It ran out in four or five days; the process started all over again. There was always household tension related to this chore. It was so much work that the women would dread it and put it off as long as possible. The result of not having sago in the house-- the men became hungry and grouchy. The men were not above beating the women to get them to go get sago. The washing of sago was one of those routine chores that became the focal point for resentment and power struggles within Wagu households.

After the hard work of collecting sago, they had to protect it.

Everything from the rats, the dogs, and even the people would steal it if given the chance. There was usually at least one person near the house watching the food at all times. The standard method of keeping the dogs away was to beat them with a stick.

The other food that was hard to keep was meat. Once it was cleaned and cut up, it was placed on smoking racks over the clay oven fireplace in the middle of the house. Cockroaches were allowed free reign over the food; everything else was kept away by the constant effort of the women.

By far the hardest thing the women of Wagu were facing was the fact that their babies were not living more than a few months. The Wagu men believed that women actually gave birth to killing *kwonu* spirits and could direct them toward people, preferably in enemy villages. Local women who became senile or mentally disturbed were often executed in brutal ways for being witches and sending *kwonu*.

The menstrual blood and birth fluids from the women were viewed as spiritually dangerous. For this reason, during menstruation, women were isolated outside the village. They were confined to a small shack consisted of four spindly posts with palm fronds thrown over them, and the fronds covered a four foot by six-foot platform of sago bark just above the ground. The women would sit on a bark slab to catch the blood. The hut was surrounded by mosquitoes and flies because of the smell of blood. Sisters or co-wives could bring them sago, but little else. They went through a special washing ceremony before they could return to the house and family, and eat normally.

This same hut was also used to give birth to their babies. The woman would squat and hang onto a vine hanging from a tree branch or the roof of the birth house. They were attended to by an older mother who acted as a midwife. Often other women in the village joined to cheer them on. Their bodies were hardened from the hard labor of their lives, so births went fairly quickly. They would rub stinging needles on the woman's belly to distract from pain during the process. The midwife used spring water carried in a bark bowl from a nearby spring to wash away the blood and a flint stone knife to cut the cord. The men would stand at a distance and listen for the sounds of the newborn crying and hear the announcement of the newborn with anticipation.

More than twenty-three healthy babies were born to at least eighteen women between 1956 and 1964, but not a single one lived more than a few months. The mourning and wailing of new mothers losing their babies was devastating to the people of Wagu, and they struggled to understand. Had someone in the family offended a *dafa* of a man that recently died? Was the baby killed by a *kwonu*? If so, who might have sent it on them? They had no way of knowing, but they were sure there was a spiritual cause and it was likely a *kwonu* or a *dafa*.

It is difficult to imagine how desperate things were in Wagu, especially for the women. When their babies died, they cried out in grief and frustration. If they cried too long, the men beat them and threatened them to keep them quiet. There were literally no children around to give them hope and motivate them to keep on striving. The only things keeping the women going were the pain in their stomachs from hunger, the fear of death, and the fear of reprisal from their husbands if they did not work.

Naba was a very quiet, thoughtful man, and felt the pain of those around him. Naintu's wives were like sisters to him, and he grieved with them when Yamu lost two babies a year apart. He was sensitive to their plight and cried out to the *dafa* spirit of his father for help. One night he had a very strange dream, a dream of a white man coming to the village with a book. He heard distinctly, "The book will give you the answers you are looking for." Naba awoke full of hope and excitement and told the village the dream. The village wondered about the dream and some began to hope.

Chapter 7 – The Mission Field

Dye family mission photo

As the date approached for Wayne and Sally to leave, the one thing that was not coming together was the financial support. The boat reservations were made, the barrels were packed, the house was closed, they were ready to step out in faith, and they were still short the minimum support pledges required by Wycliffe to make the trip to the field. At each step, they had just enough money for the next step but never more. This was a huge struggle for Wayne; he questioned God's providence and their calling. Sally continued to encourage him to pray and claim God's provision as promised in scripture. They continued forward believing that God would provide.

God showed His mercy to the exhausted family when they missed the train after Edith drove them to Chicago. The next train to California only had a more expensive secluded compartment available. The cabin was an amazing upgrade. They were able to take turns sleeping and entertaining the children. The last-minute switch to the nicer room was taken as a blessing from God and confirmation that they were doing the right thing. Their cooler full of food lasted them all three days to San Francisco.

Some of Wayne and Sally's friends from InterVarsity, Warren and Doris Moos, were living near San Francisco. Wayne and Sally stayed with them while they were waiting for the boat's departure. Warren was now a physics professor at Stanford University. He and Wayne discussed how blind faith could lead one up a dead-end street. Warren was not supportive of them leaving for New Guinea without sufficient funds.

Still no funds came. Wayne was discouraged by the fact that money had not come in and was questioning if all this was their own idea and that God was not behind it. He reasoned that God could not have sent them because He was not coming through with the money. Wayne believed they must have been "hearing" their own inner wishes. He saw this as a dead-end street and feared that they must not have heard God. Sally was insistent that God would come through, and they just had to trust him. Wayne's name sake, Uncle Wayne Trueman, was living in Red Bluff, California, and invited them to come speak at his church. Wayne and Sally agreed, both to see him again and in hopes of raising a little more money for the trip. As Wayne was preparing the talk, his mind kept going to Exodus 14 where God leads the people of Israel to a dead end for His glory. When he spoke to the church that night, he said that he was convinced that God sometimes does lead people up "dead-end streets," that He was going to come through for them, and they were going to get the funds they needed to get on that ship to New Guinea.

On August 31, 1963, just hours before boat launch, Warren and

Doris took Wayne and Sally out to a nice dinner at Fisherman's Wharf. Wayne wrote a short note addressed to his parents, Rev. & Mrs. Marion Dye. It read:

"Hi Folks,

I'm writing this at a nice restaurant here at Fisherman's Wharf. We board Oriana in one hour. Since I called you [asking for prayer for our finances]:

1. GBC [Grace Bible Church] promised us $365 during the next 3 months
2. Warren and Doris pledged another $350 during the same period
3. Strathmoor-Judson Baptist promised us $250 right away plus another $70 per month support
4. The ship changed us [from two rooms at opposite ends of the ship] to a four-bed cabin at a rebate of $225.

So we are going to the field free and clear. Praise the Lord. Love Wayne and Sally"

For Wayne and his friend Warren, this was a real test of faith and a proof of God's ability to provide. The total sum of the money that came in those last few hours before the boat left exactly met the dollar amount the mission board had insisted they have before departure. Warren and Doris became faithful supporters of Wayne and Sally after seeing God's hand in bringing in the exact amount of funds needed by the mission board.

While there is no mention of it in any of the letters, Sally's recollection of that first few days on the high seas was miserable: their family of five cramped in the little cabin getting their sea legs while cleaning up vomit. But by the time they sailed into Honolulu on September 6th, they enjoyed the beach and were in much better spirits. The ship would travel to Sydney via Fiji and Auckland arriving September 17th. Both Wayne and Sally would describe the last ten days of the trip as a much-needed vacation, with lots of opportunity to rest. The Oriana had a nursery for the children available much of the day, and a special dining room with foods for young children. There were many special activities the children enjoyed. A formal meal was served in the evening. Wayne and Sally found another missionary family and the two couples took turns eating and babysitting each other's children as they settled to sleep.

The ship's small pool was filled with seawater pumped from the ocean directly; the temperature varied with the latitude of the ship. They enjoyed the pool when they were in tropical waters, but as they headed south to New Zealand the cold Antarctic currents cooled the Pacific Ocean enough that swimming was no longer an option.

Wayne's letters to Edith mention a costume party in which Edie dressed as a pumpkin, Joy as Peter Pumpkin Eater, and Tom as a prize fighter. They also mention watching Swiss Family Robinson in a movie theater. They witnessed a changing of the governor ceremony in Fiji. During the bus tour of Auckland, New Zealand, Edie and Joy enjoyed seeing sheep for the first time. Wayne has always dreamed of going back there sometime and seeing more of that unusual island.

They spent a week in a missionary guest house in Sydney at the coldest time of the year. They waited there for the weekly scheduled Boeing 707 flight to Port Moresby in New Guinea. Both Wayne and Sally independently wrote home about those days in Sydney being the most miserable of the whole trip. They did not have clothing for cold weather and there was no central heat in the guest house - just a fireplace in the living-room where they could dry and dress the children after a shower. They put the children between them in their bed to keep them warm. The couple running the guest-house were not helpful and just wanted them to toughen up. The food was very foreign to the kids, and that combined with the cold made the time there frustrating and miserable. They did take the kids to the zoo and to see the Sydney Harbor.

After flying to New Guinea, they found the atmosphere at Mapang Guest House in Port Moresby was much better. On a return visit to Port Moresby in 2008, Sally would say the Mapang Guest House did not change much since she first arrived in 1963. It still stood out as a place for guests to enjoy good service, good food, and great people. Sally's letter to Val describes the Moresby Guest House as "paradise." Wayne, Sally, Edie, Joy, and Tom really enjoyed the ten day stay in Port Moresby waiting for the next flight to Ukarumpa. This time was longer and more relaxed than they anticipated and provided much-needed rest for both parents and kids. There was a shift in the focus of the letters as Wayne and Sally began to anticipate mission work and their field assignments. They were eager to get to the jungle and start their translation.

The island of New Guinea is the largest of a collection of volcanic islands in the South Pacific. It is one of the largest islands in the world and is an incredibly harsh and rugged place. The tallest peaks are over 16,000 feet (4,900 meters) high, and most of the river valleys or deltas are covered with either swamp or dense tropical rain forest. The northern tip of the island touches the equator and the southern tip almost touches the northern tip of Australia. The proximity to the equator along with the size of the mountains places it near the top of the list of wettest places on earth. This ruggedness kept the interior of New Guinea largely isolated until World War II. *Lost in Shangri-La* by Mitchell Zuckoff is a well-written documentary of an attempted plane crash rescue in the mountains of New Guinea that gives a glimpse of the challenges explorers faced in the interior of the island. The rugged mountain ranges of New Guinea proved to be a formidable barrier that helped the Australian Coast Watchers stop the advancement of the Japanese Imperial Army during World War II.

Politically, the Islands of New Guinea were divided a number of ways depending on when in history the political maps were drawn. The Dutch, the Germans, the Japanese, the British, and the Australians all had claims to portions of the islands at different times. When Wayne and Sally arrived in 1963, the eastern half of the main island and the majority of the outer islands were a territory of Australia and were being colonized in the traditional style of a British Commonwealth. There were Australian governors, for-profit businesses, and local workers. The rugged terrain and eroding streams and rivers fragmented several million people on the island, isolating them into almost a thousand language groups living in small hamlets spread through the jungle. They distrusted, fought, killed, and ate each other regularly. The Australian government had made significant progress in stemming the violence for most of the known tribes by 1963, but it was, in fact, one of the last frontiers left on the surface of the planet.

The only practical way to move from place to place across the interior of the island was by small airplane. There were a number of airstrips built in the mountains during the war. These strips were usually short grass-covered strips and were only able to support small aircraft.

JAARS is a mission support and logistics organization that partnered with Wycliffe Bible Translators to provide flight services in New Guinea and other remote areas around the world. They scheduled flights between Wycliffe's central support base at Ukarumpa in the highlands of New Guinea and various cities and villages, including the capital, Port Moresby.

Wayne and Sally were excited and nervous as the small JAARS airplane circled and approached the grass airstrip near Ukarumpa. They could see the mission base nestled on the side of the grass-covered hill, surrounded by mountains as far as the eye could see. Ukarumpa was a community on a piece of tribally-disputed land leased from the local people and located two miles from the Aiyura airstrip and agricultural station near the town of Kainantu in the Eastern Highlands. Ukarumpa was the home base for Wycliffe Bible Translators with its growing Bible translation program in New Guinea. In 1963, this expanding missionary community was in desperate need of a nurse and a civil engineer. The base was anticipating the arrival of 65 more families in the next few years and did not have physical space to house them.

The Ukarumpa settlers had already built a meeting hall, store, saw mill, mechanic shop, school, and nursery. There was a two-way radio center which was used to communicate with the various remote areas. There was power supply to the meeting house and radio center using a diesel-operated generator. A tiny business office and mail room managed the operation. JAARS flew out of Aiyura, an airstrip across the valley. The two-mile dirt road people traveled to get from one place to another oozed with mud after the frequent rains, making daily life more difficult than it needed to be.

When Wayne and Sally arrived in New Guinea, they expected to go straight to their village and start translation. They did not anticipate the needs and complexities of the technical and political life of this remote mission base and it took them a little while to find balance in their new environment.

In a letter home to her mom, Sally described their first

Ukarumpa house as follows:

"Our four room house has a grass roof, woven bamboo walls and a wood floor, handmade furniture with linoleum on the kitchen counter. I have put up some pretty red, green, and yellow plastic curtains and tablecloth from material I got in Port Moresby. We have kerosene lanterns and stove. It is very much like the [our Michigan family] cabin."

Wayne was immediately put in charge of a crew of ten local laborers to build drainage ditches, improve streets, and lay out new spaces for the future translators heading to New Guinea. One of the early design changes that Wayne came up with was the addition of bug screen on the outhouse vents to keep the flies from spreading hepatitis. Then he began working with the Ukarumpa team to eliminate the pit toilets and replace them with simple venting septic tank-like holes, draining through the gravel soil layer nearly a foot below the topsoil. He had it covered with a wooden (later cement) platform for the outhouse to sit on. There are also notes indicating Wayne was trying to get handwashing facilities near the meeting house "to reduce the

Joy and Edie at preschool

spread of disease." He and Sally were using their combined knowledge to help stop the hepatitis epidemic sweeping through Ukarumpa.

Joy and Edie were attending preschool for part of the day, but Tom did not adjust well to morning day care. Sally generally kept him with her as she typed letters, cooked, cleaned, and helped out with sick patients at the local clinic. They soon hired a local housemaid to help clean house and wash dishes for 50 cents per day which was considered a fair wage. There are several references to struggling to learn Tok Pisin in the fall of 1963, but they seem to have mastered the basics of the language by Christmas because there is no more reference to learning Tok Pisin.

The base was small enough that the director's two-page prayer letter went to all of the supporters for all of the translators, hand typed on individual air mail posts. The November 1963 director's post that was sent to Edith and Marion included the announcement of Wayne and Sally's arrival to Ukarumpa, along with birth announcements, individual translator prayer requests, and information about various people arriving and leaving Ukarumpa.

The New Guinea Branch (a division of Wycliffe Bible Translators specifically responsible for the New Guinea region, hereafter called Branch) was the authoritative body which managed the operation in New Guinea. As a general rule, missionaries set their own agenda, subject to being redirected to meet the larger Branch mission. Missionaries were evaluated annually and given homework assignments. The pioneer mission culture was one of working together with one common goal as directed by their elected leaders. The missionaries were a blend of people from a number of home countries including Australia, New Zealand, England, Holland, Canada and USA. They were a

85

very close-knit group of pioneers using limited resources to carve out an existence in a remote environment sandwiched between two warring tribes on the edge of the wilderness.

The pioneers had a vision of growth. There are several notes and action item lists that indicate that Ukarumpa was planning for another 150 families to arrive the following year. Wayne requested prayer for what to do with all the children. In that prayer request, he stated that Ukarumpa anticipated having over a hundred school-age children by the end of the decade. All that growth meant hard work, and everyone pitched in to build Ukarumpa into the logistical support hub for all those Wycliffe translators.

One of the biggest challenges was finding tribes to place translators in that were logistically feasible to reach and were open to having guests. There are several references in the early director's posts about allocations being closed because tribes were not accepting of the translators or because they were not able to maintain vehicle access to the location. One way the team was trying to solve the tribal access issue was to build air strips near the villages so supplies could be flown in. These airstrips would be built with shovel and wheelbarrow, moving thousands of yards of dirt and cutting through jungle with axes and rock with pickaxes.

Ukarumpa was not all work. Families would regularly get together for base-wide desserts, share meals and have skit nights by a campfire. The Dyes' first Thanksgiving was celebrated with a large feast for the new families living in the circle of grass huts waiting for houses to come available. This meal was prepared in the traditional pit-oven style called a *mumu* by neighboring villagers. This involved building a large shallow pit lined with rocks. A hot fire heated the rocks to red hot. Then they covered the red hot rocks with layers of banana leaves and placed all the food on top of the leaves. They then covered the food with more leaves, water, and finally dirt. After steaming several hours, the meal was uncovered and eaten as a feast. For most missionaries living in remote allocations, Ukarumpa was a welcome escape from tribal life. The strong, supportive, Christian community there provided both logistical and emotional support to the missionaries in the villages.

The prayer letters in the fall of 1963 indicate that there was an aspect of learning to trust and wait on God's timing. Wayne in particular seems to have gone through a paradigm shift spiritually. In 1961 and 1962 he was doubting God's existence, then doubting his involvement in their daily lives. By the spring of 1964, he was clearly expecting God to help in the details of everyday life, to guide and intervene in answer to prayer. There is a shift to dependency that is clear in both their prayer letters and their personal letters.

Wayne and Sally were eager to get out to their own village assignment. Both wrote home multiple times in the fall of 1963 that they were frustrated with how long it was taking for them to get cleared for a field assignment. These letters expressed frustration with the political structure of Ukarumpa. Wayne and Sally were eager to get out in the field and start their translation.

Between November of 1963 and January of 1964 Wayne traveled on several language survey trips. These are excursions into remote areas to find new language groups to reach for potential assignments. This involves a process of studying what is already known about a people group, asking locals lots of questions, and hiking through an area asking more questions and eliciting lists of words in order to compare the language with others.

Wayne wrote home about surveying one such group in November. Lyle Scholz, a translator friend working near Simbai, had heard of a newly-contacted group in the mountains to the south called the Karam. Wayne reported that they were too remote to hike in with small children and there was not enough ground for an airstrip. That was a disappointment; both Wayne and Sally wanted to work with a remote people like these.

Wayne began to plan a tribal survey to the Gahom people for December 28, 1963. To reach the Gahom people from Ukarumpa, Wayne had to travel by JAARS flight 2 hours to Ambunti on the Sepik River near Wewak.

Wayne's flight was met at the airstrip by Neal Kooyers. Neal and Martha were translators for Wycliffe and were the leaders of the local group of Wycliffe missionaries working in the East Sepik region. Wayne had been working with Neal on the trip logistics. Neal provided the canoe and the supplies. Another translator in that area, Robin Farnsworth, hired the guide Yambonam, a man from Yambun village with wide local knowledge. Yambonam was familiar with the Sepik River that they would go up to reach the mouth of the April River. However, not even Yambonam knew much about the remote jungle area where Gahom village was located.

Wagu Lake from JARRS plane

Sepik motor canoes are less than two feet wide; people and equipment sit along the center keel to keep them stable. Everything that is not sealed in a waterproof container gets wet either from the tropical rain or spray from the wake formed by the canoe carving its way upstream. At Ambunti, the Sepik is approximately a mile wide and averages a hundred feet (30 meters) deep. It winds through seven hundred miles of Sepik lowlands like a giant brown snake. Most of the Sepik Plain is swamp with an occasional hill or strip of land rising above the marsh. The one exception is Mount Hunstein. This mountain is a five thousand-foot (1,500 meters) high volcano that looms above the Sepik plain. The forest-covered ridges from this magnificent peak reach out toward the edge of the Sepik river like giant arms forming the territory of the Gahom people.

Wayne, Neal, Robin, and Yambonam loaded the 30 foot (9 meter) long canoe with supplies. The village Wayne had heard about was on the far side of the mountain and Wayne's team must travel around the peak, up the fast-moving April River to reach the tribe. He had read the government's report on the route, but actually traveling up river in this wobbly motor canoe was a whole new level of reality.

Every mile or two along the Sepik River, there is a backwater channel connecting local shallow lakes and drainages from the local hills. In the US, Wayne had bought surplus ammunition boxes left over from the war. These came in handy to put the radio and other equipment that could not handle the wet canoe bottom. The other supplies were placed loose in the canoe. When he was a teenager, Yambonam had witnessed the peace talks between the Yambun and the Genesowayagu. He told stories of when he was a boy and the Japanese occupied Ambunti. On the way up the river, they stopped at several villages, trading goods and gathering information.

Once one got accustomed to the 90 degree Sepik River heat, the near 100% humidity, the clouds of mosquitoes, the spiders crawling over everything, and the other logistical hurdles, the rainforest where the Gahom people live was stunningly beautiful. In the letter Wayne wrote on the trip, he described it as follows:

"The Gahom area is, to me, the most beautiful in New Guinea. One travels on a fast, clear river through dense jungle. There are game birds in sight all the time. On our short survey, we saw dozens of ducks, beautiful *guria* (Tok Pisin word for Victoria Crowned Pigeon) as big as wild turkeys, two wild pigs, innumerable hornbills, all kinds of parrots and cockatoos, and plenty of large game fish."

Wayne and his team did reach the Gahom people located in the village of Wobagus and the people did accept them in. Wayne was excited, but he was concerned about the low population of the tribal group, the remoteness of the main village, and the cost of getting to and from the language group. Sally had said she did not want to allocate to a tribal group with less than five hundred people, but during his survey he concluded that this group could be as few as two hundred people.

Two nights before, it had poured rain and filled the canoe with water. The "waterproof" radio box had 2 inches of water in the bottom and the radio had been soaked. They had tried to dry it over their camping stove, but they felt sure it no longer worked. As they traveled up the April river to Wobagus, Wayne had prayed and asked God for a sign. If God wanted them to allocate with the Gahom people, He would have to make two things happen that Wayne did not think were possible.

1. He would have to fix the water-soaked broken radio so that Wayne could call Sally on that wet radio.
2. She would have to feel excited about the allocation in spite of the size of the people group.

The next morning, the radio worked perfectly and Sally was very excited and wanted to come to Gahom. Wayne took this as clear guidance and became convinced of the decision to allocate in Gahom.

On the way downriver, Neal Kooyers said that he had heard speakers of the Gahom language living in Wagu Village near Ambunti. Wayne decided to go to Wagu to see whether they really did speak the Gahom language. When the team came on shore at Wagu, the people looked at them suspiciously. Wayne said to them, "I want to translate God's book into Gahom. Does anyone in this village speak Gahom?" Remembering Naba's dream, the Wagu people replied in unison, "We all speak Gahom." They welcomed Wayne and promised to help build a house. Wagu Village was on the edge of a beautiful lake with mountains in the background; the logistics were much better because it was less than two hours from Yambun and Ambunti.

The next big decision for Wayne and the Sepik mission team was which of these two villages the Dye family should settle in. Wayne describes this as more of a practical engineering decision than guidance from God. The Wagu village was so close to Ambunti, and the houses were better built. The people were more able to communicate with them. Wayne felt Wagu would be less expensive, an easier place to live, and safer for Edie, Joy, and Tom. Wayne wrote a four-page letter at the end of the Gahom survey. In that letter, he had already moved past the decision of where to allocate and began to describe details of what the house would be built out of and what equipment he would need to buy to live in Wagu.

Chapter 8 – Wagu Village

A 1964 allocation map produced by the Branch shows fifty-seven translation allocations around the country including Wayne and Sally with the Gahom. The New Guinea Branch was informally organized by regions. This structure was necessary for coordination, communication, and logistics. It was self-imposed more by necessity than by a drive to control or direct. The structure provided accountability and formalized a way to make sure missionaries in remote places were ok and not getting overwhelmed by their circumstances. The overall Branch was run by director Jim Dean and Associate Director Ray Nicholson. They assigned most decisions about the Sepik region to Neal Kooyers, who was also a Sepik Translator. The director required monthly reports from each field team. These reports were typed on a standard two-page form. The reports answered questions related to how much progress had been made on the translation, what the translators had read in their devotions, and about their health. The Director or Associate Director would visit each site and give an annual evaluation of the Wycliffe members working there. In this respect Wycliffe was run very much like a business with the product being language translation. The expectations for productive progress was high and was the primary objective of the allocated team. The daily experience of the missionary in the field was that he was on his or own in remote pace with only a radio as a life line to the outside world. The organization was there to make the mission work successful and make sure that the field was functional.

The real support network that made remote allocations possible was the field team. The Sepik team at that time included Neal and Martha Kooyers, Phil and Lori Staalsen, Bob and Joanne Conrad, Robin and Marva Farnsworth, and a pair of single women Velma Foreman and Helen Marten. Most of them had built a local style house in a village of their language group. The

Conrads were living on a small houseboat of Western materials and pontoons made of local canoes. There was no safe place to anchor it at Ambunti, so they were keeping it at Yambun village and allowing the Farnsworths to use it whenever they were away.

SIL translators were each supported by a base partner at Ukarumpa who prayed for them, checked in with them on the radio, bought supplies for them, and generally stayed in touch with their lives. They communicated through letters sent through regularly scheduled JAARS flights and two-way radio conversations. For safety and logistic reasons there were two times a week in which the teams in the field had to check in by radio and report on recent events. There were daily announcements that you could listen to but it was not mandatory. From a practical perspective, the sun caused so much interference to the radio that the only time one could get good reception was early and late in the day. Electricity was at a premium because batteries had to be charged with gas generators, so teams used kerosene lamps at night. The practical result was that the missionaries had a narrow window of time at dawn and at dusk to communicate on the radio. The group of Sepik translators functioned as a team and provided each other with practical help, emotional support, advice, and spiritual support. The friendships forged in these early days would last the rest of Wayne and Sally's career.

Wayne and Sally's support team were Hap and Gladys Skinner. Hap was an Australian Mechanic who ran the repair shop at Ukarumpa and often help build houses or airstrips or whatever needed to be done. His wife Gladys was a nurse from the midwestern United States. They met while Hap was touring the United States on his motor cycle. They have their own adventure story written in a book called *Tales of Two 'Happy and Glad' Skinner*, by Hap and Gladys Skinner.

Wayne and Sally were eager to get to the Sepik and began assembling their supplies, but Director Dean had one more project for Wayne before he green-lighted him to go to Wagu. One of the translators, Ken Davis, had a remote location that took a 10-hour rugged hike to reach and was working on an airstrip. His wife had a knee injury and could not make the trip, so Ken convinced members from the five local villages to help him build an airstrip for easier access. Ken worked with a twenty-person crew donating their labor from the five villages. Under Ken's direction, the village men carved the airstrip out of the jungle with axes, picks, and shovels. The construction crew did not even have a wheelbarrow. The crew was hauling dirt to grade the strip using a burlap sack. Ken had been working for two months and was making progress, but needed a wheelbarrow to speed things up. He also had some civil engineering issues and needed help. Director Dean decided Wayne was the right guy for the job and sent him out with the supplies to help finish the airstrip. An excerpt from the instructional letter listed among other things the need to cut through a hill that is 15 feet high and 100 feet long. Wayne was met at the trail head by local national who helped haul the new wheelbarrow and supplies the 10-hour hike through the jungle. Wayne worked with the people about five days, living in a small shack at the side of the strip. He showed them how to use a wheelbarrow and surveyed the airstrip to lay it out more carefully.

Ken came down with hepatitis and was not healing. Wayne radioed the Ukarumpa doctor for guidance. Because of the serious nature of the disease, the doctor said Ken needed to be hospitalized and Wayne needed to be quarantined. The base doctor was worried that if Ken tried to walk out himself, it would do permanent damage to his liver and possibly even kill him. Ken weighed over 200 pounds. Wayne hired 16 men, 2 teams of 8 to take turns and haul him out on the rugged mountain trail on a stretcher he had made with nylon rope, a poncho and local poles. Wayne and Ken were then quarantined in a Lae hospital until they were cleared to return to Ukarumpa. (In those days, it was normal in New Guinea for everyone to contract hepatitis as a small child, when the disease is actually mild, and thereafter built up a resistance to the disease.)

While Wayne was building the airstrip, Sally was preparing for Wagu, collecting and shipping supplies to the Sepik team in Ambunti. Everything she had dreamed about since Junior High School was finally coming to pass. She was excited, but she was also scared. The reality of taking her 3 little babies to a remote jungle village finally was sinking in. So many friends and family had warned her not to take them to the jungle, but she and Wayne still felt confident it was the right thing to do. Now, they were seeing others doing it. Yet, they knew there were so many things that could go wrong. They were going to live with Stone Age cannibals in tropical jungle full of hepatitis, malaria, tuberculosis, poisonous snakes, crocodiles, spiders and cockroaches (her favorite).

When Wayne and Sally arrived with the children to go to Wagu it was wet season and the Sepik River was at flood stage. The Hunstein River was clogged with floating grass islands blocking the primary route to Wagu. Wayne and Robin had to develop an alternative plan. The plan was to fly from Ukarumpa to Ambunti, take a motor canoe up the river to Yambun, then cut across the flooded banks of the Hunstein between the Sepik and Wagu Lake. This would shorten the trip from seven hours of hard poling through sharp grass to 2 hours of intermittent motor and hand poling through the shallow flooded grass land. This route became known as the Yambun Cut Off and became the route of choice whenever it was possible.

Sally sat in the kitchen of the Conrad's house boat drinking Koolaid trying to adjust to the stifling heat of Sepik plains. High heat and humidity were a huge contrast from the cool 75 degrees of Ukarumpa. She was struggling to come to terms with what was about to happen. Little Tommy tugged at the hem of her dress and she looked down and smiled. "What am I doing," she asked herself?

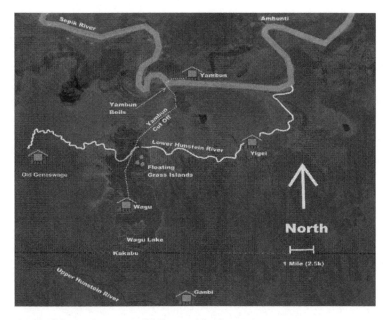

Map of the region around Wagu with places river routes

But the day finally came, for Wayne and Sally to have many helping to get them, the children and the supplies and building materials into three dugout motor canoes. These canoes were all 30 or more feet long, but less than two feet wide. Now they poled their more fragile load, shifting their weight automatically to balance the canoe with the skill of men who have lived in them since boyhood. They traveled up river near the bank to a location called the "Yambun Boils". There is a submerged rock shelf in the bottom of the Sepik River at this location that can flip boats, but these men knew how to use the various whirl pools and cross currents created by the rock shelf to cross the half mile wide river and head into the flooded lowland towards

Wagu Village.

The 12 Yambun men used long paddles that were carved out of buttress roots and paddled standing up like modern paddle boarders. Wayne stood toward the middle of their canoe, awkwardly trying to balance himself, trying to mimic the local men, not realizing they were having to counter balance his actions. Sepik women normally sat down and used a shorter paddle similar to a traditional canoe paddle. Wayne had been an experienced canoeist back home in Michigan, but standing in the middle of the jungle swamp trying not to fall in while dodging vines and poling through swamp was a whole different story.

Tom drinking as Joy watches

Edie, Joy and Tom huddled around Sally towards the back of the canoe behind the baggage. They looked around with wonder at all they saw, seeking reassurance in the strange new environment. They had been covered in mosquito repellent an hour ago, but sweat had washed it off and they were slapping at the clouds of mosquitoes inside the canoe. Sally handed them biscuits or mouthfuls of water from a canteen as they got restless during the four-hour trip.

Every time the canoe bumped into the grass or scraped against a branch it would drop in spiders, grasshoppers, flies and mosquitos. Many brown mosquitoes sat on the moist backs and legs of the sweating men, gorging themselves undisturbed, then sluggishly hopping away, dragging their bloated reddened bodies into a dark corner to digest their meal. These men seemed completely unaware of any pain, engrossed as they were in getting safely to the destination far across the marsh.

The innumerable jungle vines twisted up through the sago palm trees. Some had sharp barbed tendrils reaching back down to snatch hold of the unwary traveler. Every tree and vine seemed to reach out toward canoe with long spiny thorns. The man at the prow deftly slashed at the overhanging branches with a bush knife as the canoe advanced through the narrow channels between several small lakes. Robin ran the outboard motor when he could, but most of the time there was too much grass and vines and they had to pole.

The shade from the sago trees were a welcome break from the intense sun that blazed over the great marsh of the Sepik flood plain. The little cotton sun hats on the children and Sally-s straw hat were no match for the intense tropical sun. While the discomfort and fear were intense, they still managed to notice the beautiful things around them. The white clouds floated low on the horizon, contrasting sharp against the blue sky, the black water, and the green jungle. The water in the small lakes was covered with blue and pink water lilies, tiny fringed white flowers and lovely green rosettes floating upon the water. Thousands of birds of two dozen varieties flew from the front of the canoe. Others ran away across the two-foot diameter lily pads. Cormorants, parrots, hawks, egrets, and eagles fled from the larger trees as they approached. It seemed that God had sent an unusual number of his creatures to welcome them to this forgotten land.

As Sally soaked in all this, she could not shake the turmoil in her mind. She was full of fear and doubt, and she struggled to hide her inner struggle from the little children nestled around her. They were depending on her for courage.

She pondered the warnings from well-meaning supporters back home. One couple had even offered to care for the children for Wayne and Sally for the first five years in New Guinea. Wayne and Sally had always felt right about bringing the kids to the village. They were pleasantly surprised and happy to discover how many missionaries had children and how much accommodation the Branch had for them. The reality of the jungle before her brought her back to legitimacy of the concern raised by people who disagreed with their choice. A number of Wycliffe translators had contracted hepatitis in the past year. Others had severe malaria. Anything could happen. What would they do if the canoe tipped over in this crocodile-infested swamp? The life jackets they had ordered had not yet arrived.

Sally meditated on the words from the Psalms: "No evil shall befall you…. No plague shall come nigh thy dwelling."

As they pushed past the last of the marshland and entered Wagu lake, she looked up and saw the beauty once more. The Hunstein mountain range was reflected in a giant five square mile mirror. The jungle was every shade of green that you could imagine. Her mind jumped back to junior high where she sat in the church basement and listened as a missionary told her story. She remembered the last slide of a mountain. At that moment, the words came clearly back into her mind "Beyond those mountains are people who have never heard about Christ. Someone needs to go there." She remembered the quiet voice in her heart. "Sally, I want you to go there."

Lillys on Wagu Lake

There was a sudden awareness of rightness and a calm came over her. She was fulfilling that calling she had heard all those years ago. She along with Wayne, Edie, Joy, and Tom were right where God wanted them at that moment. They were here to show God's love to these people and translate God's Word into their language. They motored through a deep channel lined with struggling trees, then crossed the lake to the wooded hill to the right side of the lake where there was a small cluster of brown thatched houses near the lakeshore and framed by the dense green jungle. Two smaller houses clung to the hillside well above the others. The upper one was much larger and was likely the government officer's house. That is where they would be staying until they built their own house. The government had required each village to build a house for officers and policeman to stay in when they make occasional visits. It is also available for other visitors like Wayne and Sally.

Wayne and Sally had brought the materials to build a bush house that would look just like the villagers, the same size and with the same basic materials. They felt this would help them fit in and build relationships better.

As the boat pulled up the shore several village men came down to greet them. The greeting seemed warm but reserved. The guides helped the children and Sally across the small gap of

Wagu village taken in 1967

water between where the front end of the canoe ends and the land, as the tip is too narrow to be stable when placed on the shore. The girls were eager to be ashore, even though there was little level ground to walk on. The women who had stood to the back, greeted them, and assisted them as the girls clambered up the steep earthen steps carved out of the hillside. Little Tommy clung to Sally as she joined the procession of willing men each carrying armloads of their supplies. More and more people joined them, assisting all they could as they followed their guides up to the *haus kiap* (government mandated guest house) nearly fifty feet up the side of the hill.

The smaller house Sally saw from the lake was a strange hut. Sally could see dark carved figures in the darkness. This must be the spirit house, a focal point of the spirit worship. Sally glanced away, afraid to offend the village men on her first day, as she had heard that women were forbidden to see inside.

From the just outside the *haus kiap* was a picturesque view of the lake framed by several kinds of palm trees. White egrets fed among the water lilies along the western shore. Beyond these the marsh reached far into the distance until another range of hills pushed out above it, forming a background. The deep blue sky with wispy white puffs stretched overhead.

Spirit carvings in the men's house

As people carried their supplies into the village, and the children were occupied in making new friends, Sally observed the people more closely. The village men's clothing ranged from new shirts and trousers to a string tied around the waist supporting a piece of cloth dangling down in front, to trousers, most of which were torn in several places and looked as if they had never been washed. The women all had on new clothing, obviously not worn often. They were shy and quiet as they climbed up to Wayne and Sally and began to quietly admire the children.

These unique people had shy smiles and a gentle touch as they reached out to the children. They were so different from the more exuberant highland people they had encountered. Sally felt more comfortable with this shyer, more reserved people. Sally still cringed and shuddered at their filthy bodies and scaly ringworm covered skin, but tried her best to hide the fear she had for her children. After putting down their loads, the people were very quiet and mostly just stood and watched every movement of the white family that had just plunked down in their world.

The lack of children was immediately obvious, like a scene in the movie "Chitty Chitty Bang Bang." Where had all the children gone? There was one very thin little baby and a few pre-adolescent boys and girls. Sally wondered if they had hidden them out of fear of the white people. There were dogs, scrawny mangy dogs, all skin and bones and very small. If the dogs got too close to the luggage someone would yell and swing at them and they would quickly dart a few feet away.

The frames of the houses were held up on three center posts cut from trees twenty to thirty feet long and buried deep in the ground. The long roof post rested on these forked post, reinforced with heavy vines and covered with platted palm leaves. Six shorter forked posts held the lower edge of the roof on either side. Next to these were another set of at least nine shorter posts that held up the floor frame. The bark platform was raised off the ground at least four to eight feet, depending on the slant of the hillside. The walls were made from vertically placed palm branches lashed in place by vines and the roof was a sloping pitch covered with sago palm leaves neatly stacked and lashed to cross beams cut from the rain forest. The house was built completely from materials found in the rainforest and lashed together with vines. The village houses had a single four-inch diameter log with some notches carved in it for entry, but the *haus kiap* had what appeared to be an attempt at a Western style ladder to use to climb in to the house. One of the rungs of the ladder of the house broke as soon as Wayne tried to use it. A young man named Begai Wuna, pronounced "Bug-eye," offered to fix it. Wayne found him a hammer and some nails. He had learned to use Western tools during the three years he had spent on a coconut plantation.

The bark floor was full of cracks and gaps, twice Tom's little foot slipped through a crack scratching his leg and causing him to cry. The people laughed. Wayne and Sally visited with the few people brave enough to come inside with them and tried to remember their names. The children wandered around the space and investigated.

Taken later but show a typical "House Kiap"

Most of the Yambun men took two of the canoes back before dark, but a few men stayed behind to help Wayne with the language and cultural barriers, and with house construction. Wayne and Sally were left with one motor canoe to work with.

That night the whole family attempted to sleep inside the nine foot by twelve-foot nylon room net they had bought second hand at Ukarumpa. Sally had made a sturdy room net with her sewing machine back in Ukarumpa, but it was smaller, so they used it for a separate cooking and eating area. Wayne and Sally had spread out a large sheet of plastic on the bark floor then a foam mattress for the kids and an air mattress for them. There were many mosquitoes inside the net, and they took some time with a flash light to kill them all. Wayne and Sally had brought a hand pump which they filled with DDT (dichlorodiphenyltrichloroethane) to spray the mosquitoes in the house, but they were not able to locate it that first night. The children struggled to fall asleep. The bites they had obtained on the journey were now itching and it was hot. Sally wiped down their bites with denatured alcohol which helped cool them off and calm the itching and slowly they each in turn gave in to their exhaustion.

Begai listening intently.

That evening Begai came back with another young man he introduced as Naba Sawini. For Naba, this was the answer to prayers to the spirits and the fulfillment of his dream. He was eager to learn the secrets of the white man's book. Wayne and Sally spent an hour writing down names of people and items at hand, using the phonetic script they had learned in linguistics classes in Oklahoma.

As Wayne and Sally lay in bed that night they said a brief prayer. "Thank you, God, for getting us here safely." It was interrupted by the noise of light scratching sounds of an animal in the house and then the sound of slurping, a growl, and then, the shrill squealing and scrambling of two dogs fighting. Wayne got up and chased them out of the house, tried to hide everything they thought they might be interested and went back to bed. In the morning, they discovered a chewed-up bar of soap he had left out. The dogs would end up being a serious problem. These hungry dogs found a way around every barrier attempted to keep them out of the house. When Wayne blocked the doors, they shinnied up the posts in to the house. When he blocked that route, they climbed in the cracks in the walls. Finally, after they blocked all the routes, the dogs howled outside the house all night. Sally was bitten once trying to chase one out of the mosquito net. This terrified her; she did not know that there was no rabies in New Guinea. The dogs were the first of a whole series of logistical and practical issues that faced them as they learned to adapt to their new environment.

There were two springs near the village, a small one fifty yards from the house and a larger one three hundred yards from the house. The village women hauled water from the springs in bark basins. All the water for drinking had to be boiled, which heated up the already hot house. Wayne and Sally were hesitant to keep asking for more water, but neither was capable of hauling it themselves. In the humidity, everyone needed to drink a lot to in order to stay hydrated. They kept the use of water to sponge baths, cooking, and drinking.

Sally wanted to keep the kids' mosquito bites to a minimum so she kept them in the nine by twelve screen room. Even a trip to the poorly constructed pit toilet would result in several dozen mosquito bites. The framing around the toilet pit was so flimsy looking that Sally was afraid she would fall in. She definitely did not trust that her preschoolers would not fall in, so they went to the bathroom in a sturdy bucket with a make shift box lid which Wayne created.

Wayne started to focus immediately on the house. They planned together on materials needed; the men spent several days in the forest gathering the many needed poles, palm stems and leaves, and bark for the floor. After gathering materials, they worked diligently each day on the progress of the house. The Dye family lived on the food they brought with them. You can only fix canned mackerel and spam so many ways before you lose your appetite. After a week and a half everyone was exhausted, grouchy, mosquito bitten and Tom had a fever. Sally saw evidence that the early bites were now getting infected and she was worried that fever was a sign that the infection was getting worse.

Their hardest moment came a day or so later when a thunderstorm blew in after dark. The wind whipped their fragile sleeping net against the rough poles and tore a long strip. For the next hour Wayne tried to keep waving and slapping the mosquitos from their children while Sally worked with needle and thread and a flashlight to stitch it together. Then more swatting, spraying (with the now found spray gun) and applying alcohol to the many new bites.) The same thing happened the next night; the wind blew in; they got up and patched it again. The net was too fragile for the Sepik winds. Wayne and Sally were at the end of their ability and the striving was not helping.

Wayne and Sally's view of the purpose of prayer was very different at this point in their lives. Prayer for the skeptic is a vehicle, like meditation, to clear your thinking and refocus. For the person who sees God as a loving and all powerful, ever present deity, prayer is a plea for God to intervene in their lives.

Wayne believed in God, and he was beginning to buy into the idea that God could and would intervene on his behalf, but he was still did not want to bug Him with the little things that he could solve himself, much like an employee who was hesitant to ask his supervisor for help, but would prefer to solve it himself. For Sally prayer was a constant dialogue with God and she often grew frustrated and impatient when God did not intervene immediately on the family's behalf. Sally was putting her babies at risk to do His work, and she wanted His intervention to make it safer and less miserable for her babies.

Most of the other translators, and in fact, the majority view of the evangelical community of the 19600s, was that God did not actively engage in intervention in people's lives. For them prayer was a vehicle to hear God's voice and direction for guidance, but they did not expect miraculous intervention into life's circumstances.

For Wayne and Sally, the meaning and purpose of prayer would change over time. But in these first few exhausting weeks, prayer took the form of simple pleas for help in their daily lives. After praying, unusual solutions would come to mind to smooth out some of the logistics in their daily lives.

Sally began to take the children down the hill to visit with the women for a few hours a day. She connected with a woman named Maki. Maki was short and thinly muscular, she was shy, but her eyes sparkled and her smile was contagious. She tried to teach Sally the names of things.

After two weeks of misery and exhaustion, Wayne and Sally concluded that it would really be better all-around for Sally and the kids to return to the Conrad's house boat back in Yambun with Jo Ann until the house was built.

The Yambuns who had been helping Wayne were happy to take the family out and get home for the weekend. The canoe trip out was absolutely miserable. At one point the canoe plowed in to a grass island and they were attacked by clouds of mosquitoes. The kids lost it and began to scream. They screamed and cried for the remaining one hour and a half trip to Yambun. Everyone was exhausted, stressed out, and grouchy. Wayne remembered back on those weeks and said, "We were prepared for martyrdom, but we were not prepared for misery." Sally left the village feeling very defeated and over-whelmed. Sally wrote the director in late April requesting help and asked about the option of returning to Ukarumpa.

When they arrived, Jo Ann Conrad was there but Bob was at May River bringing back someone to help them with the language. It was common practice for Wycliffe translators to share their stuff including houses. Jo Ann could see how defeated Wayne and Sally were and set about to cheer them up. She took the kids outside to play in shallow flooded area where the Sepik River had overflowed its banks; she washed off the grime from the trip and they enjoyed the cool water. After that, Joanne helped Sally bake a cake for Joy's birthday and they had a little party. This helped Wayne face returning to the village feeling a little hope that Sally and the kids were in good hands.

In Yambun, Sally felt a little more comfortable about letting the kids out of the house. There was shallow water around the houseboat and the children looked for every opportunity to get back in it. The village had puppies, baby chicks, and baby pigs; Edie could not resist going to see them. The Farnsworths, a Wycliffe family living in a house in the same village, had a brand of bug repellent that proved to be significantly more effective than the thirty tubes Wayne and Sally had brought. Jo Ann, Sally's hostess on the houseboat, helped with the kids, and Sally enjoyed some rest.

As she pondered the events that led her to this place, she thought back to her initial calling. She thought about her nursing training and her meeting Wayne. She wondered about Wycliffe and her striving to get here. She thought about the people that had given and sacrificed on their behalf, her mother-in-law and her mom who worked so hard back home to make sure they had the money and stuff they needed. Why was it so hard? They had been obedient, why did God not intervene and make it easier?

Sally studied her Bible, seeking some promise. One afternoon she read, "Oh thou afflicted, tossed with tempest, and not comforted, behold I will lay thy stones with fair colors, and…all they children shall be taught of the Lord, and great shall be the peace of thy children…This is the heritage of the servants of the Lord." (Isaiah 54:11, 13,17). Sally concluded that she was indeed following God's will and He would care for them. Over the next few days her courage and resolve returned. She would return to the village as an act of faith that God's hand was in it and do her best to manage the safety and comfort of her children in spite of the difficulties.

Chapter 9 – Working out the Kinks

The Hunstein River from Wagu Lake to Ambunti was a part of a complicated system of lakes and rivers that requires explanation. The Hunstein River below Wagu Lake was fed from four sources, Wagu Lake, the upper parts of the river itself, other lakes along the sides of the river, and the Sepik River into which it empties. Depending on rainfall and the resulting water level in each source, the Hunstein could get its flow from any combination of these. Normally, its main flow was from upriver with some from the lake. If the Sepik River was high, the whole area was flooded, and there was very slow flow through all of them. When it was low, most of the flow came from the upper Hunstein River. Occasionally, the Sepik would be higher than the Hunstein and water would flow up the Hunstein, sometimes even getting as far as Wagu Lake. The flow pattern could not be accurately predicted even by people living in the area.

The behavior of the marsh grass further complicated the situation. The lakes were often filled with a combination of rotting vegetation and silt. The resulting tannin caused the water to be black. Grasses, trees, and shrubs sent out shallow roots in the mud when the water level was low and became entwined with each other into large dense root balls. The soil under these was mostly rotting vegetation. Its decomposition produced gasses that were trapped under the porous vegetation and roots. When the water level rose in the rainy season, these root balls would float and create floating islands, which could be as small as a car or as big as a soccer field

During wet seasons the lakes were high and quiet, and the floating islands of grass went where the wind blew them, sometimes floating into the Hunstein River and becoming jammed. A canoe could still be pushed past those islands, though it took time and effort. During a dry spell, the Sepik water level would drop rapidly, the lakes would empty, and the current would push the floating islands into the Hunstein River, making travel much more difficult. The impact of grass islands on the Hunstein River channel would prove to be a serious hindrance to travel between Wagu Village and Ambunti.

The water levels in the Sepik River had dropped to the point where the Yambun cutoff was no longer viable. Wayne left Sally and the kids at Jo Ann's and returned to Wagu via the Hunstein River to test whether they could get through. He and the Yambon men who had come with him went to Ambunti to pick up supplies, then up the Hunstein River. They used their long, forked poles to push the boat through marshy areas. It turned out to be a seven-hour nightmare with all of them pushing through numerous grass blockages amid clouds of mosquitoes. At one point in a moment of frustration, Wayne counted one hundred mosquito bites between the top of his foot and his shin. He made it to Wagu completely exhausted, but surprisingly rejuvenated. All that exertion had released some of the pent-up tension he was experiencing trying to manage the house construction and the impossible situation for his wife and kids.

Wayne set to work re-engineering the house to better protect the kids from bugs and dogs. He still wanted space to meet with the people, but he added screen doors between the living room and kitchen to cut mosquitoes. He added full and half height screened windows to allow more light in and gain access to the beautiful view of the lake. He also added a box toilet (a bucket in a box that could not be tipped over, but had to be dumped in an outdoor pit toilet daily). He had spent months imagining the laying out the house, doing quantity estimates of screening, building paper, nails and hardware, and arranging shipment of materials from Lae, Wewak, and Ukarumpa all based on the original design. He was very concerned that the design changes would use too much material and he would not have enough

114

to finish the house.

He wrote the following in his May 1964 prayer letter:

"God planned our delay to Wagu, which was frustrating to us then, so that we arrived in Wagu at a time when the men were between hunting seasons and had very little to do. Every man in the village worked on this house.

Secondly, our building material orders were thoroughly mixed up. I miscalculated on nails, we had to change our wall plans, and thus needed more building paper, and the screening had not been delivered when we came to Wagu. But we were able to complete our house without delay (in less than a month), and with one foot of building paper, five feet of screening, and less than a dozen nails left."

This and other statements in the letter show a belief on Wayne's part that God was behind the scenes in spite of his effort, and that God was intervening on his and Sally's behalf.

The house was a huge upgrade. The whole lake side was open screen; the house had a living/greeting area with benches at the door, a large kitchen with cooking and eating areas, two bedrooms, and a bathroom and three by six storage shelves. Wayne had screened in the space under the house as a play area for the kids so they could be outside and avoid being bitten by clouds of bugs. He had constructed a plastic sheeting rain harvesting system on one side of the roof which drained into three of the fifty-five gallon drums they had brought their stuff in from the US. He piped the water into the shower stall to fill the bucket shower, as well as to the kitchen sink so they had drinking water that did not need to be boiled.

Progress on the house went quickly, and within a few weeks he was ready for Sally and the children to return to Wagu. In the morning scheduled radio call, called a "sched," Wayne said he was almost done with the house, he said the screens were up and he could sleep in the house relatively dog and mosquito free. Sally began to prepare to return. The Sepik was no longer in flood stage and the kids safe swimming area was drying up. They would have to take the Hunstein River route through the grass choked, mosquito infested, channel. The memory of awful trip out started to rush back into Sally's mind.

Wayne also dreaded the trip. He decided he might be able to make it easier by hiring men to go with him ahead of time by that route to clear some of the grass. Wayne and his team struggled hard to cut up the grass, but their effort felt like a complete failure. A full day's work and they had accomplished almost nothing. Unbeknown to them the natural hydraulics of the river systems was starting to have an effect. The Sepik was falling more rapidly than the Hunstein and the velocity in the canal was increasing.

Sally was resolved to return regardless of the difficulty. Bob Conrad was back and volunteered to take her and the children with Yambun men to help push through the grass. She quietly prayed that the trip would go smoothly for the sake of the kids. She was dreading it, but felt confident that God wanted her back with Wayne in Wagu. The combination of Wayne's team's hard work cutting key tangles and the increasing speed of the current had started to clear the grass out of the river channel. Sally and Bob's trip back into Wagu took seven hours, but was much easier than expected. They quickly settled in to the house, relieved that it was much better than the nightmare accommodation of the first trip.

The people began to bring bananas and squash for sale just to check out the house. Wayne and Sally loved the fresh food. They even started get fresh fish and an occasional pig leg from a fresh kill. The kids loved their new playground and were much more relaxed. They had been given a puppy in Yambun that occupied a lot of their time.

The Wagu people did not have a name for their language. They

Wagu Inhabitants in 1964 Male heads of family	Wife [Recently deceased]	Children *adopted	Language, Village
Yalfei Yemsu TUHIYU	Yagumei		Genesowayagu x2
Yagu TUHIYU (bro)			Genesowayagu x1
Naintu SAWINI	Yamu	Yasiyo * SAWINI	Bahinemo, Yigai x3
	Kaba Yugehi		Genesowayagu x 1
		Naba * SAWINI	Bahinemo, Yigai x1
		Ginwa * SAWINI	Bahinemo, Yigai x1
Kedul Gogomo SIMBA (changed to WABUFAYO)	[Midi]	Wamini SIMBA	Kakilu-Bitara x2
		Sakwal SIMBA	Kakilu-Bitara x1
	[Doma]	Moyali SIMBA	Kakilu-Bitara x1
		Leito * SIMBA	Kakilu-Bitara x1
	Bagu	Sufa	Nikilu x2
		Bowi	Nikilu x1
Bagi HUBAFU	Mali	Dwali	Bahinemo, Gahom x3
	Maki	Bayei *	Nikilu x2
Wanegi HUBAFU	Mongwi		Bahinemo, Gahom x2
	Batko YISIBAYO		Genesowayagu x1
Wafiyo DEHI	Faisowa		Behinemo, Gahom 2
Begai WUNA			Bahinemo, Gahom 1
Magofa WUNA	Bakwei YAGENEFAYO		Bahinemo, Gahom 2
Mature Men 9	Wives 10	Girls 5, Boys 6	Total population 30
LANGUAGE TOTALS:	Bahinemo: Yigai 5		4 language in 1964
Genesowayagu + 5	Gahom 12 = +15	Kakilu-Bitara +5	Nikilu 5 = WAGU 30

Best available information about who was in Wagu in 1964

used village names

that did not identify the tribe or language. Because Wagu village consisted of people who spoke Gahom, Nikilu, Kakilu, and Genesowayagu, the decision of which language to teach these crazy white folks had significant political and strategic impacts on the village. The decision was definitely influenced by their statement to Wayne during his first visit that they spoke Gahom. That was not the only consideration, however. It was Yafei's land and his village, and it is likely that the people deferred to him to make the choice. We can only speculate as why and how the choice was made, but the name Gahom was chosen and it stuck. One consequence of this choice was that the original language of Genesowayagu eventually died out completely. It is worth noting here that Wayne and Sally did not

117

understand the reasons and implications of the people's choice of Gahom for the translation until ten years later.

The Gahom language eventually became known as "Bahinemo" meaning "our language" a term all the villagers could identify with. In fact, many of the village translators were learning Gahom/Bahinemo right alongside Wayne and Sally. This made the language learning and translating process much more difficult. But Wayne and Sally were good linguists and the people were eager and together they made forward rogress.

Several days after Sally returned to Wagu, she was baking cookies in her new kitchen when Yamu and Kaba (the two wives of Naintu) came to her door. At Sally's invitation, they came into the entry room. Wayne had built several benches and a medicine cupboard with a table. The intent of this room was to entertain and it was intentionally darker like the village houses. They called it the people's room. Sally invited them to come through the second screened door into the kitchen.

Yamu had a large string bag or bilum strung across her forehead and draped across her back. She was much shorter than Kabu and leaned forward to balance her load. Sally suddenly realized that the only baby in the village was sleeping in that string bag. She was laying on a smooth bark mat, nestled in the woven crib. Sally passed them sugar and flower drums to sit on and Yamu brought the baby forward into her lap. The women had on the traditional grass skirts. These were a pleasant reddish-brown color of raffia-like texture, but they wore brightly colored cloth blouses gathered at the neck falling full over their bosoms, with puffy gathered sleeves, a style sold in Most New Guinea trade stores. Their faces could have been the faces of any women back home. Yamu had the long black quills of a rhinoceros beetle placed in two holes pierced in the top of her nose.

At just over five feet in height, Kaba was tall for a Wagu woman. The muscles in her arms rippled with strength as she moved them, but her broad smile and the soft curves of her face showed that she was feminine Her black tightly curled hair was trimmed short and the back of her neck shaved up in a neat line just above the ear lobe. Kaba didn't wear the rhinoceros beetle quills, instead she had some kind of bark neatly placed to keep the pierced hole intact. There was a neat hole in the sep-

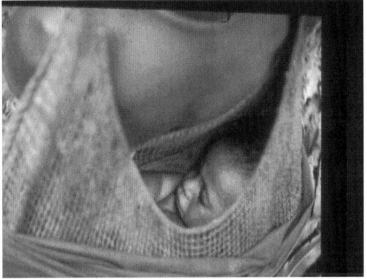

Typical baby in a Bilum (string bag)

tum of her nose, apparently for special dress-up occasions.

Yamu and Kaba were amazed at the running water from the faucet in the stainless-steel sink that took up the whole end of the counter next to the stove.

They watched fascinated as Sally took the different ingredients from the countertop "rat proof" cupboard Wayne had bought from the base joinery shop and shipped on the plane. Sally started the pressure primus stove by lighting some alcohol in the little spirit pan underneath the burner to vaporize the kerosene enough to burn with a blue flame. After the stove was lit she had to pump up the pressure to get a good hot flame. Then the cookies were shaped on the cake pan and put in the stove top oven.

The little baby girl started to cry, so Yamu lifted her blouse to nurse. After the baby had nursed a couple of minutes they lifted her from the string bag. Kaba gently by her arms as the baby smiled and stretched, her legs bouncing up. Both the women laughed and cooed as they watched over their precious little girl. She was naked except for a little multicolored beaded necklace around her neck. As she started to urinate, Kaba quickly held her out over the bark floor until she was finished. Then Yamu asked for water and they poured it over the baby's skinny legs and buttocks and then over the floor as she continued to hold the baby out. Apparently, they found this the easiest way to keep her clean in this hot humid climate. Sally asked her name, but they had apparently not given her one.

Yamu and Kaba got up and began looking around into the other rooms, a sign that they wanted to be shown the house. Sally took them past the work bench at the far end of the kitchen. It was presently the center of Wayne's work on finishing up the cupboards and furniture, and was also where Wayne lit the kerosene pressure lamps. Across from this was a little hallway with a borrowed two-way radio. They were fascinated with this. They wanted a peek at all the Western amenities Wayne had built into the house.

Sally was finally feeling like this was a home and she could be a host to these people. She was also learning how incredibly nice it was to be married to a civil engineer when you are living in a remote jungle far from civilization.

Although Wayne had lined the floor and ceiling with paper and the walls with screen wire, there were still occasions when unwelcome guests found their way in. The most common were the large jumping huntsman spiders. They were intimidating but not too harmful. The most dangerous small creature in the house was the centipede. One day a red and yellow centipede crawled out of the bark floor inches from Tommy's toddling feet. Its four-inch long segmented body wiggled quickly under another section of the floor. DDT spray finally drove it out again. Wayne and Sally found and killed several. They had been warned that the pain from the centipede sting was excruciating so Sally kept an eye out and used the hand pump of DDT liberally

A week after Sally's return to Wagu, Director Dean arrived for an overnight visit to the village. Sally's plea for help had caught his attention and he came to investigate. Robin Farnsworth also came back. Thanks to the hard work of Wagu people and the natural increase in flow from the Hunstein, they had a smooth two-hour ride up the Hunstein River in a motor canoe, with no grass to block their way. With the new house built and the river clear of grass, Director Dean did not experience the hardships Wayne and Sally had. He wrote a letter to Wayne and Sally a few days later, in which he asked them to spend more time in scripture and in prayer. It was likely not the director's intent to shame or frustrate, but Wayne and Sally were frustrated that the director did not understand how tough things really were and felt shame over their supposed failure to handle the hardships of the village.

Chapter 10 – Illness, Healing, and Power

That evening, Robin Farnsworth, who was a little more in tune with village life, noticed a sick man that Wayne and Sally were not aware of. Robin informed Sally of a man with pneumonia who needed antibiotics or he would die. Sally went to investigate and was directed into the dark house in the late afternoon. Maki and Mali greeted her quietly as they patted out the sago powder on the clay plates over the fire. She was directed to the back of the room in the usual Bahinemo way. There was an old man lying by the smoldering fire at the back corner of the house. Several people started yelling excitedly at him as she approached. They passed a ragged piece of cloth quickly and someone hurriedly tucked it around his naked emaciated frame. But the bearded old man in the darkness only forced a grunt of recognition as he breathed with noisy rattles and coughed occasionally.

Sally struggled with her nursing training to figure something to do. This was so different from the big regional hospital where she had worked in Michigan. She had no supplies, and everything was so filthy. Her first instinct was to get him to their house, but everyone objected. She could not let him die so she prayed - "God help me to do the right thing to save this man."

Sally gave him a shot of penicillin each day along with cream of wheat gruel. After about a week or so, he walked slowly up the stairway of the new house. She hardly recognized the clean-shaven man with a trim haircut who held out his hand. Joyfully she shook the hand of this middle-aged man who was on his death bed a week earlier. The Wagu people were convinced that without Sally's help old Kedul would have died. In East Sepik culture this was a huge show of power; and She began to gain respect as a healer.

Wayne and Sally were still not very sensitive to how deadly and unforgiving the tropics was, and they missed some deadly symptoms in Yamu's little girl. When Yamu, Kaba, and Naintu came with the baby complaining that she had a fever and was not going to the bathroom correctly, Sally could not figure out what was wrong. She gave some aspirin and sent them home again. A few hours later she heard the wailing. She thought it was a howling dog at first, but soon she recognized the sound of a woman's agony. Yamu's little baby was gone and the family quickly left the village to grieve. Wayne and Sally inquired about the cause of death, and the village blamed it on the *kwonu*. Sally was heartbroken.

Her fear for her own children returned. A few days later Tommy got sick with a fever and Sally could not figure out what was wrong. She tried to force malaria pills down him, but he kept crying and spitting them up. She used cool rags to keep him cool, but for several days his fever was over one hundred and two. They started talking about leaving the village.

Sally finally prayed, "God, please keep your promises in Psalm 91 and protect Tommy from any serious illness. Make the Enemy take his hands off him and make him completely well. Thank you, God, for hearing us - Amen." Sally felt a moment of overwhelming relief of fear and dread as the fever left. Tom got up and began to play.

The events of that second month in Wagu began to change Sally's thinking about the spiritual and physical world. She began to see God as someone who was ready and willing to answer prayer. She began to look for evidence of a possible link between physical illness and spiritual causes. This journey and exploration between the physical and spiritual would last the rest of her life.

Wayne's faith was encouraged and there were more references

to God and his providence in his letters home. He also began to be more sensitive to dark spiritual forces.

There are no written accounts of how the Wagu people felt when the Dyes arrived. All the Wagu people who were there are now dead or were too young to remember. We can make some observations based on the few stories we have been told, knowledge of their culture, and an understanding of their world view. Belief in ghosts and spirits pervaded their thinking. They believed that dreams were messages from the spirits. Wayne and Sally were told multiple times about ghost sightings and omens of death.

The Wagu people dealt in terms of power: power over circumstances, power over life and death, power to bring food, and power to protect from evil. Power was demonstrated in action, words had little meaning in their culture. Money was a brand-new thing to them, only a few of them had it, and it was only useful for exchange with outsiders. The currency of the Wagu people was mutual obligation.

To the Wagu people, Wayne and Sally were very powerful; they had power over all the things that mattered. They had food, they had tools which overcame the tough aspects of living, and they had the ability to heal. Naba's had a dream predicting their arrival was a significant omen.

In the fifty years since Wayne and Sally's arrival there have been very few things that prompted the level of hard work and cooperation that the people of Wagu put forth in the first two months of their arrival. Their interest was clear; they welcomed Wayne and Sally and helped them in every way they could. They hauled water for them, they provided material for the house; and shared their meager food supplies. Wayne and Sally did not fully understand the extent of the tribal exchange and obligation, but were aware of its existence. They chose to pay for services rendered, but it was never clear how much was enough or how the village valued money. The exchange of goods and services is essential for relationship and there was a desire on Wayne and Sally's part as well as on the people's part to build a relationship.

A skeptic might say that the people were motivated by a desire to deposit exchange credit with powerful people for future return on investment. The spiritual person might say that they did it because of Naba's dream and the hope it promised. The truth is probably a combination of motives which varied from person to person and time to time. Whatever the motives, Wayne and Sally reaped the benefit of the Wagu people's hard work and resources.

It is also clear that Naintu was hoping Wayne and Sally and their medicine would save his little girl. He had instructed his wives to learn their ways and take their medicine. He had fathered so many children and all of them had died. He was sure that this girl would be different because Wayne and Sally were there. He lost hope when his girl died; he took his wives and left the village to grieve. He did not just grieve the death of his daughter; he grieved the death of his hope.

Chapter 11 – Joining the Tribe

Naba and Begai did everything they could to teach Wayne and Sally the language, believing that Wayne and Sally were the fulfillment of the message Naba had had in his dream. They hung on to the hope that the knowledge in this book would keep their babies from dying. Others came and went, depending on the circumstances, but Naba and Begai were always there to help and to learn.

Wafiyo taken many years later

Wafiyo (wa fee yo) Dehi, was another young man who had been off to the plantation. He began to show in interest in the new foreigners in the village. He had shown promise on the plantation and had been given extra training about planting and growing coconuts. He was a quick learner and had a lot of personal drive. Upon returning to the Sepik he had taken several jobs as a river guide for foreign anthropologists and scientists, and therefore had some ability with Tok Pisin. Although he did not hold either of the government appointed leadership positions, luluai (headman) or tultul, (spokesman), Wafiyo was already beginning to stand out in Wagu. Time would prove that Wafiyo was a socially skilled leader who would ultimately compete with Yafei for the position of power in the village. When Wafiyo arrived back in the village, he joined Naba and Begai in doing what they could to help Wayne and Sally.

When the Director saw Wayne's creative work on their house, he decided to add him to the crew building the guest house at Ambunti. The missionaries were relying heavily on government charity in Ambunti, and the Branch was worried they were wearing out their welcome. The Ambunti house would serve as a logistics hub to support the translators and would house supplies. It would also serve as a place to stay near the airstrip overnight while coming and going to the remote locations. Often it was difficult to make the trip from Ukarumpa to a remote village in one day. The house would also reduce dependence on the government resource and use of government warehouse to store mail and materials. Director Dean decided that Neal Kooyers, Phil Staalsen, Robin Farnsworth, Wayne Dye, Hap Skinner, and Jack Bass were going to build the Ambunti Guest House. While the men worked on Ambunti house, Martha Kooyers joined Sally in Wagu. Sally learned a lot about the Sepik people and raising children there from her.

At one point during this stay in Wagu, Edie was playing with some dolls that Wayne and Sally had brought from Ukarumpa. Edie was pretending the doll was her baby and taking care of it. Naba, who was watching, interrupted Edie's game to say, "Now the baby dies." Edie argued back, but Naba casually insisted, "All babies die," as if it was an obvious statement like "the sky is blue." Naba added for Sallyls hearing, "The women are so busy sending evil spirits, they are too busy to take good care of their babies." For Sally this punctuated the certainty that Wagu people had grown to accept infant death and witchcraft

128

as normal.

Wayne returned to Wagu after successfully completing the Ambunti guest house. He brought back Phil Staalsen's shotgun with plenty of shells. They commissioned Kedul's son Wamini to hunt for them, and they started getting fresh meat regularly after that. Wayne had also commissioned the people to build a large canoe out of cedar wood. Even in the rainforest, a large diameter cedar is a rare find, so the Wagu people kept their eye out as they came and went hunting and gathering food.

Yafei leaving to hunt pigs with his dogs

Back at the village the dry season was upon them. The beautiful lake had dried up into a stagnate mud flat. There were fish dying from the loss of oxygen, floating and causing an awful stench. The largest problem was the water supply. The three rain barrels were running low and the rain was not coming. Sally pressed Wayne to pray for rain. She saw water as a basic need that God promised to supply His children, but Wayne was worried about praying for rain because the impact on others that might not want rain. He eventually agreed that the need was great, and without water they would have to leave the village. For several weeks in a row they would pray for rain and it would come and fill up their drums, then as the drums went down again, they would pray again. Even though they would see rain clouds and lightning in the distance most nights, it only rained on Wagu the nights they prayed. Wayne was so impressed that he roughed out a statistical estimate on paper just to make sure that this was not possible. He concluded that the link between the rain and prayer could not be chance.

They were making progress with both the language and with connecting with the people. It was getting to be mid-July, and they were trying to figure out what they could do for a break from the hot dry season and the dreary muddy lake. Then, one of the hunters reported finding a log he thought would make a perfect motor canoe. The tree stood at a place called Ganbi, one day's hike away from the village on the Hunstein River. They described it as a beautiful place with good water and plenty of food. The people encouraged them to join them at Ganbi. They promised to help meet their needs, including building them a bush house and hunting food for them.

Wayne decided to go and investigate Ganbi. He came back a few days later with plans to bring Sally and the children. They packed up their food and supplies and headed out on their jungle camping trip.

Villagers carried the stuff and the children while Wayne and Sally walked. The jungle was beautiful. They saw a cassowary feeding in the river on the way. Naba shot it with the shotgun and everyone cheered; there would be a feast in camp tonight.

The men put up a sapling tent frame for them, and Wayne helped them cover it with a tarp. Wayne and Sally put up two double mosquito nets for them and the children. They put air mattresses and foam on the ground covered with sheets. On later trips they learned to sleep on a bark platform to avoid flooding, chiggers, ants, and the many other creatures living on the jungle floor. The people all slept in a bush house that was nearby.

They camped on the banks of the Hunstein River, but it was hard to believe it was the same water. The slow moving black swamp water which flowed near Wagu this far upstream was a fast moving, crystal clear stream with deep pools full of fish. The banks were draped in flowering vines; the bright orange cluster of blossoms were spectacular. Birds of paradise, eagles, hawks, and horn bills flew back and forth across the stream. Turtles and Monitor lizards hunted in the shallow waters. The air was cool and there were very few mosquitoes. The former Genesowayagu Village residents had given up much of the beauty of their land to be nearer the outsiders and their tools on Wagu Lake.

The next day Wayne took Sally and the children to see the men cutting the canoe. The making of canoes was new to the Wagu people, who were used to the mountains and had not spent much time on the lake. Furthermore, they had never built a large motor canoe. Wayne was concerned and wanted to have a part the process. He had heard stories of poorly built canoes, especially crooked or curved ones. Neal had advised him to stay involved. The men happily beat their axes in time as they carved out the interior log they had just cut down.

After visiting the site of the canoe Sally took the children with Maki to the place where the sago was being chopped. The women sat on one edge of the split-open sago palm log scraping it with stone axes. They sang as they worked, with each stroke they broke off a small chunk of the soft core of the palm trunk. They let Sally try also. It did not take long for her to get blisters on her hands and give up. Maki placed this heavy bag of sago across her forehead into the groove that was formed into her skull from years of caring heavy string bags. The water-logged sago starched drained through the string bag and oozed down her back. Sally was amazed at how daintily she carried the load over the rough trail, never stumbling or missing her footing. Her small muscular frame glistened with perspiration as she walked.

Taken years later - This is the stream where they camped

Naintu, Yamu and Kaba had returned from mourning the little girl. They joined the group at Ganbi and helped gather food from the jungle. Sally was amazed at the women's skill with a bush knife as they cut down trees and gathered food. The three women took care to attend to Sally and the children as they walked through the jungle after them.

The jungle was where the Wagu people were most comfortable, and food was abundant. They shared what they found with Sally, encouraging her to taste everything. They found a large mound of leaves and dirt about five feet high, like a giant compost pile. They got down on their hands and knees and carefully dug through the pile. Yamu produced a large egg from the pile. It was about the size of six hens' eggs. One egg would feed the whole family. They kept bringing these eggs. Wayne and Sally wondered how they found so many eggs in the pile of

132

leaves. Later, they discovered that the eggs were from a New Guinea variety of the megapod bird, meaning "big feet." Instead of sitting on their eggs, they rely on the heat generated from rotting vegetation the male places in the mound to incubate the eggs. Each chick starts digging his own way out of the dirt after hatching two months later. When all the food everyone gathered was put together, there was a great feast in Ganbi again that night.

The people were sharing their world and were generous in every way. Wayne, Sally and the children were having a genuinely good time. During that trip, Sally learned to cook with hot rocks, make sago, and use fern leaves as both plates and napkins.

The children's favorite pastime was swimming in the shallow cool water near the edge of the stream. Butterflies would land on their bright clothes thinking they were flowers. After a week, they had run out of Western food, but Sally and the kids were not ready to leave. Wayne decided to hike out with two of the men for more food.

Wayne had a festering wound that had started back when he was working on the Ambunti house. Neither Wayne nor Sally really understood the danger of blood poisoning from a tropical ulcer at the time, so they had not paid close enough attention to the wound. They had treated the wound topically and it always seemed to respond well, but never quite healed. The physical exertion of trying to keep up with the men on the hike back to the village from Ganbi may have worked against his body's attempt to isolate the infection. Whatever the cause, he arrived back in Wagu with a raging fever and had to stay an extra night to recover.

A couple of days before they were to drag the canoe out of the bush, the men began to discuss a name for it. Wafiyo came over to the Dyes' camp and announced, "We are going to name the canoe after the *wulyal* who occupies this area of the forest and guided the growth of the tree." Wayne and Sally had intended to let the Wagu people name the canoe, but became alarmed when they wanted to name it after a *wulyal* spirit they worshipped. Wafiyo went on to tell how it created that part of the forest and provided food for their trip. This sparked a discussion between Wayne and Sally; they agreed and told Wafiyo, "We cannot name the canoe after a *wulyal*." The people were very unhappy, because this was their normal custom.

That night, Wayne, Sally, and the children all had terrifying nightmares and woke with an overwhelming sense of foreboding and fear. Suddenly the jungle seemed frightening with its weird noises. They cuddled the children to quiet them, and the whole family huddled together, feeling small in the dark jungle. The children went back to sleep, but neither Wayne nor Sally could shake the oppressing fear and vision of their simultaneous dreams. Wayne and Sally discussed it and decided to pray that God would take control over any evil forces. The fear and the sense of oppression disappeared and they went back to sleep in peace. They both agreed that there was a connection between refusing to name the canoe after the forest spirit and the experience in the middle of the night.

Wayne and Sally decided to name the canoe after their son Tom. In Bahinemo the name came out "Doma Tom" and essentially meant the canoe named Tom. The people all loved Tom and accepted the name. When the canoe was finished and painted, Wayne wrote "Doma Tom" on the prow.

During the two weeks at Ganbi, Wafiyo initiated an adoption ritual which made Wayne his brother. Wafiyo simply said to Wayne, "We have tied many vines together. From now on we will call each other, Leikim" (vines tied). They were to refer to each other by this relationship name, rather than their personal names. This simple adoption was more significant than Wayne realized. It became a link that made both Wayne and Sally members of the tribe and established family relationships all around. Wayne was now related to every person with the same relationship as Wafiyo had. Sally was related to everyone in the same way Wafiyo's wife Faisowa was. Naba became a son. Bahinemos would have followed through by finding out what to call each person in the village, and use all those names rather than their given names. Wayne and Sally did use the name "Leikim", but did not know enough to follow through according to custom. They still used given names, rather than these new relationship names for everyone else. Even this failure was overlooked by most everyone.

In many ways, this two-week trip to the jungle was the true beginning of a lifelong relationship between Wayne and Sally and the Wagu people. Much like a summer camp bonds a group of scouts, or "hell week" bonds football players, the Ganbi experience bonded that group of twenty people and forever changed how they viewed each other.

For the Dye children, and likely the Wagu children, the Hunstein River Valley where Ganbi is located became a favorite place. They would all say later in life that it is truly one of the most beautiful places they have ever experienced. For Edie, the trip began a lifelong passion to protect the Hunstein range and the people of the Hunstein Range. As a result of her persistence, it has become an official PNG forest preserve. This story was written up by Edie an article in National Geographic Feb 1994 and later in her book *Rendezvous With a Rainforest*.

Eventually, paradise had to end and they all returned to Wagu. Wayne was in a lot of pain and his fever kept coming and going.

His health was declining. Sally was getting worried. She was still worried about the possibility of an unknown disease that was killing people in Wagu. Yamu's baby had died with very few external symptoms and now Wayne was getting sicker and sicker.

While Sally was struggling with how to treat Wayne, Wafiyo and Naba came to him sad and forlorn. Wafiyo said, "Wamini has seen a ghost in the form of a pig that disappeared before his eyes. It is going to kill someone in our clan. I am sorry I brought you into my clan, because it looks now like it will be you." Their explanations did not make sense to Wayne and Sally. Something about old Waga's spirit being angry. They believed that Wayne's fever was a sign. They had thought at first old Kedul would be killed, but since Sally rescued Kedul, the spirit might be angry at them and take Wayne instead. When Wayne had done the survey in January, he did remember an older man named Waga in Wobagus. Waga had seemed in good health, but had died in the last six months.

All of this began to weigh heavily on Sally. She pleaded with Wayne to pray with her over his illness. He argued back that his was a medical issue and she had a nursing degree and should use her medical knowledge. He pressed her to recognize the large skilled organization God had provided for these purposes. He argued that God wanted them to solve this themselves. Sally was desperate and at the limits of her knowledge. Giving up and afraid for Wayne's life, she activated the emergency protocol. Her anxiety was apparent over the radio, because the support person manning the radio sounded the alarm. They could not contact any other translators in the area, so Director Dean contacted the government in Wewak. It was a classic case of "telephone" (or radio in this case). The leading government official in Wewak first heard the message on the New Guinea regional news, which had listened in and reported it. The radio report said, "a white family in Wagu were all sick and the government was not doing anything to help." The government reacted immediately by sending a speed boat to Wagu.

Before putting everyone to sleep, Sally gave Wayne her last penicillin shot and a treatment dose for malaria, just in case. The kiap's group arrived around midnight and evacuated the whole family. Wayne, Sally and the children spent the rest of the night as guests in the government officer's home in Ambunti.

By morning Wayne's fever broke, but the doctor was already on his way on an early morning charter flight from Wewak, to take the family to Wewak hospital. Wayne was treated in the Wewak hospital for the infection in his left ankle. Director Dean flew to Wewak at the request of the Austrailian Government and had a very unpleasant meeting in which he had to plead for permission to allow Wayne and Sally to stay in the country. The government officer was very concerned about having a hapless Western family in such a remote and dangerous place and was threating to revoke Wayne and Sally's visa.

Director Dean flew back with Sally and the kids via JAARS to Ukarumpa while Wayne remained in the hospital. On August 2, 1964 Wayne wrote a very interesting twelve-page letter to his mother while recovering in the Wewak hospital. In truth, he was probably sicker then everyone realized. Blood infections from tropical ulcers are, in fact, life threatening. He had responded well to the intravenous antibiotics. Still, the government representative called it a false alarm and wrote a nasty letter to Director Dean for wasting the government's time and money. Wayne was mortified; Wycliffe was embarrassed. Wayne was on the next scheduled JAARS flight from Wewak to Ukarumpa.

It had truly been an intense four months, but Wayne and Sally were hooked. They were finally living their childhood dreams of being missionaries in a faraway land, making a difference for Christ by bringing the gospel to a lost world.

Chapter 12 – Perspective and Hope

To really understand the Wagu people's perspective on the events the let up to Wayne's evacuation it is important to review their understanding of spirits, described in chapter 1.

Soon after the Dyes arrived in Wagu in 1965, nineteen Nikilu people moved in, increasing the Wagu population to fifty.

Immigrants to Wagu in 1965 bringing total to 59 population

Male heads of family [6 recently deceased]	Wife [Recently deceased] (close relation)	Children *adopted Also unmarried men	Language, Village	
(Naintu)	(Yamu) newborn	Genwaha	Wagu-Yigai	x1
(Magofa)	(Bakwei) newborn	Yemsu Jim	Wagu-Gahom	x1
[Dwali BIDA]	Wana	Waga BIDA / Bibogu BIDA	Gahom	x3
[Bofki WABUFAYO]	[Wasiya]	Gwami WABUFAYO	Nikilu	x3
Kikweli WABUFAYO	Kwinei Gida / Faya Balei	Kokomo* Yagena-fayo-Wabufayo	Nikilu / Kakilu-Bitara	x4 / x1
Sika WABUFAYO	Duba Wani HUBAFU [newborn]	Tawa, f / Wabi, m	Nikilu	x4
[Miyo YEGENAFAYO]	[Gubasowa]	Besi YAGENEFAYO, m	Nikilu	x1
[Bega YEGENAFAYO]	[Tufenku]	Kenyofo, YEGENAFAYO / Kwofi YEGENAFAYO	Nikili	x2
	[Wasubul]	Kiyawi YEGENAFAYO / Wemseli,YEGENAFAYO	Nikilu	x2
		Bawi,* f.	Nikilu	x1
[Sika YISIBAYO]		Kereniyo YISIBAYO / Batko, f. YISIBAYO	Nikilu	x2
[Waku FINIYAFU]	Nabi	(Bayei*f. by Maki)	Nikilu	x1
Mature Men 9 + 2 =11	**Wives 10 + 5 =15**	**Girls 4+5=9**	**Boys 6+12= 18**	
LANGUAGE Totals 1964-65	Bahinemo: Yigai 5 +1	Nikilu 5+20=25	1964 = 32 +27=59	
Genesowayagu 5+ 0=5	Gahom 12+4=17+5=22	Kakilu-Bitara 5+1=6	TOTAL WAGU 1965	

The Nikilu group included only two married men with two wives each. The others were nine men and four young women in their teens and early twenties. One of the young men, Kiyawi, quickly engaged the white people and began to help Wayne with whatever he needed. He learned Bahinemo as fast as he could to help with God's book. Other Nikilus who came frequently to Wayne and Sally's house were Tawa, who often brought her baby brother, Wabi, to play with Tom. Wemseli and Kereniyo volunteered help around the house. It is likely that Kokomo, the peace child that Kedul had arranged to give to the Nikilu clan in exchange for crossing their land, arrived with this group, but as a quiet observer, he was not noticed or mentioned in letters.

One of the benefits of all the added people coming to the village was the presence of young girls of marriageable age. Girls were normally married as soon as they had their first period. They stayed married until they died or their husband died. If the husband died, they would be quickly married again to another man. Single adult women did not exist in the East Sepik culture of the 1960s.

As young girls approached puberty, the men would begin to plan who was going to get which girl. The most powerful men would get the most desired girls. The clan negotiations and bride price discussion would often begin well before the girl had reached puberty, and she was very seldom consulted or involved in the decision making. Begai was gaining political power in the village and was hoping to move into his own house. He had his eye on a young girl named Bowi and was already working quietly behind the scenes to position himself to be acceptable to her clan and to accumulate the bride price.

In the spring of 1965 there were three girls approaching puberty. Bowi, Dwali, and Moyali ranged in age from 13 to 16. Because the oldest had had her period, the village made the decision to put all three girls through their traditional girls' initiation together. Their younger sisters, Sufa and Bayei, joined them in their two weeks of isolation in a small room added to one of the houses near the end of the village. During that time, the men took turns playing the flutes and worshiping the spirits. An older woman remained with them in the house and taught them the secrets of womanhood from their cultural perspective.

Young girls and women were allowed to visit them quietly, but no men were allowed. These girls were 5-year-old Edie's friends and playmates so when they were put in isolation, she went to investigate. She would visit them for several hours each day during their isolation.

At the end of the isolation, the whole village formed a line from the isolation hut to the front of the village and cheered loudly as each girl was marched from the isolation hut to the front of the village. Men and women whipped them. The girls were screaming, but the whipping continued until their backs were bleeding. On some of the girls, the scarring from initiation was visible for the rest of their lives. After the whipping, they dressed the five up, then painted and decorated them. The whole village joined together for the feast and a dance celebrationAt the end of the isolation the whole village formed a line from the isolation hut to the front of village and cheered loudly as each girl was marched from the isolation hut to the front of the village. Men and women and whipped them. The girls were screaming but the whipping continued until their backs were bleeding. On some of the girls, the scaring from initiation was visible for the rest of their lives. After the whipping, they dressed the five up, then painted and decorated them. The whole village joined together for the feast and a dance celebration.

Girls prepared for initiation - Left to Right Bowi, Bayei, Moyali, Dwali, and Sufa

The screams and bleeding backs of those girls would stick with Joy and Edie for the rest of their lives. It stands out in their minds as a fearful and traumatic experience. For the initiated girls, it was a reminder of their place in the world. The pain would last as a reminder to fall in line and follow the tribal rules.

Once the initiation was over the girls became adults and were eligible for marriage.

One morning in late February while the men were out hunting, several of the women came to Sally and said they wanted to show her something in the jungle. She could tell it was important to them and prepared for the hike, leaving the kids behind with Wayne. They walked with her up the ridge to the top of the hill and back into the forest. The route was steep; there was no path. Sally remembers falling several times, and the women had to help her up the slippery slope.

As they climbed, the women began to tell her a story about a stone they called Kwontu (which translates "demon-head"). The women were very afraid of it. Many believed it caused all the deaths in the village. As the women approached the location of the stone, they grew fearful and cautious. They pulled several tree branches back so she could see where they pointed. It was a white stone about fifteen inches long and oddly shaped. It looked kind of like the bone of a small baby with two arms. The women asked her to take it and remove it from the village.

Sally could tell by their words and tone that this was important to them. She wondered about the possibility of forest spirits, but more on her mind was wanting to help these desperate women and do what was right for them. Sally said she would pray and ask her God what to do. They kept walking as she prayed. After walking another quarter of an hour or so, Sally felt strongly that she should take the stone with her and remove it from the village. She told the women this. They returned to its hiding place. Sally picked it up.

The women kept their distance as she struggled back to the house. She fell down the steep slope and broke an "arm" off the stone. That frightened the women even more. She retrieved the broken piece. Eventually, she made it back and into the house to show Wayne. Wayne described it as smooth like quartz, but its edges appeared to be water-polished with protrusions that appeared like fingers or appendages. Wayne thought it was likely limestone or marble from a cave.

Wayne and Sally discussed what to do. They both agreed the handling of this would have spiritual implications to the people of the village. They did not want to do something that would hurt the relationship with the village. Their memories went back to the feelings of fear and foreboding they had felt in Ganbi with the canoe-naming incident. They wondered about the possibility of powerful demonic forces in this remote place. They prayed to God for protection and guidance.

Within an hour after her return, the men came back from the hunt and heard about what happened. Yafei was very angry. He ranted at the women, demanding they tell him why they had done this terrible thing to these poor innocent white people. He reminded them tha all the Dyes had done was try to help the village. He went into detail about the things the white people had brought to the village and how they were helping and teaching. He concluded with, "Didn't you know you were exposing them to death by asking them to handle this kwontu?"

Wayne holding the kwontu

Wayne stepped in and said he was not afraid of the stone and offered to pray for protection over the women and the people of the village. He said his God was bigger than the spirit of the stone and would protect him and his family. At their request, Wayne and Sally sent the stone to Ukarumpa. They took it home on furlough and then left it at the Wycliffe Center in Huntington Beach, where it was eventually thrown away.

For the men of Wagu this demonstration of power over the spirits was solid evidence, and more people began to trust Wayne and Sally. The Dyes were not aware of it at the time, but a missionary in the nearby Solomon Islands had experienced similar power confrontations. In 1967 Alan Tippett published a book called *Solomon Islands Christianity,* in which he coined the phrase "power encounter" for this kind of test of claims that God is more powerful than the other spiritual forces impacting peoples' lives. Tippet formalized using a power approach in mission work. The approach began to be discussed in Christian academic circles by the early 1970s.

As Wayne and Sally saw victories using the power approach to the *kwonu,* they saw real excitement in the people and real progress in areas of language translation and learning. The men and women of Wagu wanted to understand this power; they were hopeful that by learning about the Book, they too could

Sally's skill as a nurse helped increase the number of babies that lived.

wield the power of the foreigner.

In March Sally was invited to witness her first birth of a Wagu baby. Yamu was giving birth to her fourth child; she so hoped this baby would live. Sally was trying to see if some failure in the birthing process might be causing some of the deaths. Cutting the cord is a common source of infection. She was amazed that they actually cauterized the cord stem with live coals. Sally was also amazed at how efficient the process was, how strong the women were, and how well they managed the pain. Baby Genwaha survived.

Then in April, the women came to Sally very solemn and concerned. She followed them to the birth house, surprised because she did not think the next mother was due for a few more weeks. When she arrived, there was already a newborn infant writhing quietly on a smooth bark slab. It was not crying; something was wrong. She noticed that the umbilical cord was around its neck. Sally reached for the cord to see if it was tight. It was not. The Bahinemo believed no one should touch the baby until the afterbirth arrived. This inexperienced new mother, Bakwei, wanted to do everything right. She glared at Sally when she touched the cord.

Sally ignored the glare. She reached her finger into his mouth to check, but it was clear. The births she had observed in her training, as well as her own, were normal births with no complications. As she paused to think about her training and what to do next, she pulled away and prayed silently. Then the baby stopped breathing. At about the same time, the afterbirth came. She dared not wait any longer. Sally took control. Unwrapping the cord from around his neck, she grabbed the lifeless infant by his legs, and holding him upside down, she slapped him on the back. Nothing happened. The women gasped with astonishment but no longer appeared to object.

Sally had not had dolls to practice on in college. She had only heard the theory of infant mouth-to-mouth resuscitation in a classroom lecture. She put her lips over the baby's and began breathing into his mouth and nose, praying with each breath that God would revive the child. The young boy responded by crying out and opening his eyes. Sally paused, and he stopped breathing again. She began again, pausing to let the boy cry, then breathing for him when he stopped.

Sally's friend Maki helped her cut the cord, but it was stiff. It had no blood flow in it. The baby had been without oxygen at some point in the birth. Sally bent over the baby, observing his labored breathing, hoping he would cry more to expand his lungs. Then she had another idea. "Get the water. Let's wash him," she ordered Maki who in turn sent some younger women running. As Maki poured the cold water over the infant, he began to scream lustily. The tension was broken. Maki began to sing with joy; all joined in.

Maki handed the baby back to Sally while she washed the mother. Gradually, the boy began looking around normally, waving his arms and sucking. The new mother sat down by the fire on the freshly cleaned bark, ready to receive her baby. Gently, Sally handed him over to her. He began to nurse normally.

"If you had not been here, the baby would have died," Maki said to Sally as they watched the mother nurse. Sally responded with, "I prayed to God. He made the baby live."

The little boy was named Yemsu and later given the Western name Jim. He would become a great leader in the village, a great mind and good at figuring out how things worked.

This was a significant moment when the women of Wagu allowed Sally into their world of giving birth. Everyone came out of the birthing hut with new hope and new respect for each other. There were now four living babies in Wagu for the first time in eight years. Quinine anti-malarials, mosquito nets, and a cleaner birthing facility were a big part of the change in infant mortality rate.

By 1967, Begai had pulled together enough cash and political support to marry Bowi. The bride price negotiations were always a time of angry exchanges. These often led to physical fights as they negotiated terms, fees, and obligations. The leader of Bowi's family, Bagi, collected the bride price and displayed it on a palm stem in the middle of the village for inspection. This price usually included shells and artifacts, and later cash and pigs..

Bowi's half-brothers, Wabuwa and Waminei Simba-Wabufayo, and her new step father, Bagi Hubafu joined together to finalize and accept the bride price. The arguments continued. Other clansmen joined in and offered pieces to add until all parties were satisfied. Finally, Begai and Bowi were free to marry and settle into their own new home built on the edge of the village. Begai continued taking responsibilities for helping with the translation and leading the Bible studies. Once married, Bowi became the head of Begai's house and responsible to feed and

Bagi inspecting the bride price

take care of Begai's extended clan.

Bagai's marriage to Bowi made her responsible to care for his clan. Left to right - Wani, Hebei, Begai, Bowi, Tawa(above), Bawi, Joy, Jamey, Badi, Nulwo

Chapter 13 – Language and Logistics

Apparently having babies was contagious because Sally soon discovered she was pregnant also. Wayne and Sally were frustrated that their methods of birth control were ineffective and scared for the health of a new baby in this environment. Would their own baby suffer the same fate as the Wagu babies? Sally struggled with morning sickness. Wayne made plans to add more space to the house, including a study and more space for people to visit indoors.

In May, they took a break from Wagu and headed in the new motor canoe to visit the Farnsworths in Yambun. The water was high enough to take the Yambun cutoff so the trip was relatively short. They wanted to catch up and share the news with someone about Wagu village and about Sally's pregnancy. From Yambun, they went downriver to Ambunti to resupply before returning to Wagu.

On that return trip, they encountered a rare intense storm event that almost swamped the canoe -- six inches of water in 20 minutes. As the canoe filled up, it became dangerously unstable. They could not keep up with the bailing. Sally and the children quickly sat flat on the canoe bottom with water up to the children's waists. It took Wayne a long time to carefully negotiate the heavy current and get near the shore to wait for the storm—and their hearts-- to calm down.

Back in Wagu, they found that the added space really helped to make life easier. The biggest help was that Wayne and Sally were speaking in Bahinemo. They found it easier to communicate biblical concepts in Bahinemo than in the trade language. Tok Pisin was such a clumsy language because it had a very limited common vocabulary at that time. For example, "*bel isi*," literally meaning "stomach easy," was used for peace, joy, and contentment. There were not even words in Tok Pisin for many of the concepts written about in the New Testament. Wayne and Sally became more and more eager to use Bahinemo for daily communication, but the villagers were more interested in using Tok Pisin so they could learn it and communicate with the outside world.

Like all organizations, Wycliffe had a hierarchy of status within its membership. Only senior members of the New Guinea Branch could hold offices and have a vote in decision making. In order to become a senior member, a new member had to pass a number of qualifying tests. The tests included:

1. Analyze the sound system and create an alphabet – Wayne and Sally had accomplished this.

2. Have some degree of mastery of that language.

3. Be in good standing with no disciplinary actions against them.

4. Be "in the black" financially, meaning not owe money to the Branch.

Wayne and Sally were good linguists and very capable learners. Both had received top marks in all of their language courses. They were getting frustrated that they were not able to learn the language as quickly as other translators had. One of the reasons they cite in their letters is because the people did not speak the language around them very often . They believed this was because the people did not trust them, but in reality, the people often did not know the language very well themselves. Many of them were learning right along with Wayne and Sally. It was years later that they realized Yafei had recruited more non-Bahinemo speakers than Bahinemo speakers into the village. The fact that multiple languages were being spoken in Wagu made it very difficult for Wayne and Sally, especially when they were unaware of the other languages.

In June of 1965, Ray Nicholson came to the village to evaluate them for senior membership. Wayne and Sally failed the evaluation based on their lack of knowledge of the language and their struggles to stay in the black financially.

New Guinea Branch held an annual conference that fall. This event was core to the decision making and functionality of the Branch and all translators were called in to participate. As the date approached, Wayne and Sally did not want to return to Ukarumpa. They knew they could not return again to Wagu until several months after their baby came later in the year. They had real concerns about the new Wagu babies being left to fend for themselves without medical attention. They also were making real progress with language, and the villagers were showing interest in the content of the Bible. They wanted to bring translators back to Ukarumpa with them but did not want a repeat of the lonely time Naba had had the year before. They discussed it with the village, and Begai agreed to join Naba and fly back with them to Ukarumpa.

Naba's old village of Yigai had moved closer to the main part of the Hunstein River between Wagu and Ambunti, so Wayne and Sally had begun making it a habit to stop and visit when they passed by. On their way out from Wagu to Ukarumpa on July 10th, they stopped and found a baby in Yigai near death. They convinced the parents to go with them to Ambunti where the baby was hospitalized for anemia and soon on the road to recovery. With each successful healing, the Wagu people became more convinced of Wayne and Sally's power.

Wayne and Sally did not have their own house in Ukarumpa. There were not enough houses to go around so translators would share houses with each other. When one translator was in the village, another one would move in. If all homes were filled, like during the annual conference, people would stay in empty rooms in the children's home or even double up in each other's houses. At one point, Sally wrote home that they had moved three times in two weeks. This was logistically difficult and disruptive, and Wayne and Sally soon began writing home asking for prayer for funds to build their own house at Ukarumpa.

Not long after the annual conference was complete, Wayne and Sally passed their evaluation for senior membership with the right to vote in future conferences. They helped out in many practical ways. After their house was built in Wagu, Naba had excitedly shown Sally a book where he had drawn pages and pages of letters. Sally was amazed, but as she looked through it, there was not a word in all those pages—only letters. She took some time out each day to teach both Naba and Begai syllables, words and sentences. They finally caught the connection between letters and words. The two men worked hard and began helping Wayne record and transcribe stories that could later be used to help develop primers for teaching others to read.

Wayne was also back to working on civil engineering projects for the center as his share of "group service" each year. Up until 1965, Ukarumpa relied completely on rain water collected from galvanized iron roofs and stored in small galvanized iron water tanks. The base was seeing rapid growth and some long periods without rain. They decided that a second source of water would be necessary in the long run. Wayne's experience of nearly running out of water the year before in Wagu may have contributed to the idea of needing a water supply. There was a small stream near the base, and Wayne worked with a team to build a system of pumps, pipes, and reservoirs to provide a secondary source of water to Ukarumpa. When finished, the non-potable stream water was piped to each house, useful for toilets, laundry, gardens and other projects.

Hepatitis was still a significant problem at Ukarumpa. In early November, Sally left for Lae to give birth to their new child while Wayne stayed and looked after Edie, Joy, and Tom. In her absence, Wayne and the children came down with hepatitis. He was completely wiped out, and the whole family was put in quarantine. Sally was given a gamma globulin injection to boost her immune system. She did not come down with it.

Sally returned with baby Jamey in late November to a house full of sick people. To make it worse, Sally had thrown her back out again with the weight of the pregnancy and their many moves from house to house. Bed rest was the approved treatment for her as well. This was a very difficult time for the family. Wayne and Sally were both on bed rest with a new baby. Coworkers took turns providing a meal each day for the family until they could get up and cook for themselves again.

Another translator, Shirley Literal, came in several hours each day for about six weeks to help out with meals, cleaning, and encouragement. Wayne says this about her, "Shirley was assigned the task, but her buoyant spirit and eagerness to help went beyond an assignment." She helped move them to another house before she was given another assignment.

Edith, Wayne's mother was following these events through his regular letters and had become alarmed. She had vivid memories of her own failed mission trip to the Appalachian Mountains. In late December, Wayne scheduled a phone call with his mother to confirm for her that they were doing better.

The children were better in a couple of weeks and completely well within a month. Naba and Begai helped with some of the basic cleaning chores before they left in January. Edie and Joy helped with small errands where they could. Sally could get up for short periods to cook and do basic tasks after the move. They hired a local woman to do dishes, clean, and sweep. However, the doctor insisted that Wayne stay on complete bedrest for a full three months and then gradually return to regular tasks even after he was feeling better. Others had returned to work earlier than that and had relapsed. No one wanted that to happen to him.

In January 1966, Begai and Naba returned to the village with the Yambun translator Robin Farnsworth and sent back news from the village. There had been significant changes in the village of Wagu in their absence. Several Wagu babies had died, and the village was full of Gahom women and children fearing for their lives as a result of a raid the Wagus had participated in in November.

There is a pervasive dynamic that exists in PNG's cultural belief system that causes much, if not most, of the tribal fighting and killing throughout the country. When someone dies, the family's first assumption is that someone caused it and the death must be avenged. An internet search on "witches Papua New Guinea," brings up dozens of modern examples of this dynamic. A pervasive belief in the country is that most deaths are caused by witches (in some ethnic groups, specifically women) who send evil spirits to kill people in other clans or tribes. Therefore, when someone dies, a shaman will perform a divination ceremony in which the tribe, village, and clan responsible will be sought. The offended clan is then obligated to avenge the death by going to the designated village and killing a family member of the "witch" divined as responsible. This leads to a cycle of violence in the country that is difficult to break.

Representatives from Gahom village had come to Wagu village

155

and convinced their local clansmen that a woman from Begabegi village had performed witchcraft, causing a *kwonu* to kill their Gahom brother. The Gahom wanted revenge and wanted Wagu's help because Wagu had a shotgun.

When the Wagu men arrived together at the village of Begabegi, most of the people were out of the village, all except an older man and woman. Bagi shot them. Weeks later, the government came in with motor canoes and hauled the Gahom men and the Wagu men with ties to Gahom off to jail in Ambunti since Wagu had the only shotgun in the region. However, there were no witnesses who would speak up. Under Australian law, all the evidence was circumstantial and insufficient to convict. The twenty Wagu and Gahom men spent a year in jail awaiting trial but were never convicted. All the Gahom women and children, around twenty-five, fled three days overland to Wagu, for fear of retribution by the Begabegis.

Head man from Townsend survey in traditional dress

In late February of 1966, Wayne felt well enough to help their former University of Michigan friends Pat and Bill Townsend to go up to the Wogamus river to find a good location for an anthropology study for Pat's PHD. Pat and Bill were sponsored by the National Science Foundation and the National Institute of Health. Wayne was instrumental in helping with the allocation for the study. Wayne had been the teacher at Bill and Pat's Adult Sunday class at Grace Bible Church. Pat's degree in anthropology and Bill's degree in civil engineering provided common languages for Wayne.

In mid-March of 1966, when Wayne returned to Wagu after the Wogamus survey, the Staalsens were leaving on furlough and loaned their large kerosene fridge to the Dyes. The fridge allowed them to keep medicine, wild game, and fish as well as vegetables and cold water. Sally had not wanted to take her 4-month-old Jamey out to the village without refrigeration.

During their time away, a whooping cough epidemic swept through the Sepik area. Sally reports in a letter home that the Ambunti hospital had over a hundred babies in it with whooping cough. Wayne and Sally had made sure their own children, including little baby Jamey, were inoculated with vaccine before leaving Ukarumpa. They brought vaccine with them and vaccinated the three living Wagu babies and fifteen other children now in Wagu that had fled from Gahom.

By this time, Wayne and Sally knew to be patient and wait for the truth to come out. It took a long time, but eventually most of the facts of the raid came to light. Much later, Wayne asked Naba about the murder. Naba's response was, "It was not murder. It was one nation defending another nation the same way Australia defended itself against Japan." The significance of this in Wayne and Sally's minds was the certainty with which Naba believed that the Begabegis had sent the *kwonu* that killed the Gahom man and that they considered each village a sovereign unit. Therefore, they believed revenge against a village was defense against the attacker.

Wayne and Sally's involvement in cultural study along with their presence so deep in the jungle of the Hunstein Range made Wagu an ideal launching point for scientific and cultural studies. Others followed behind the Townsends. In the spring of 1966, Wayne and Sally were able to discuss wider language and cultural relationships with Dr. and Mrs. Meinhard Schuster, anthropologists with the Basel Museum who were studying legends and material culture. Later that year, Dr. Ruurd Hoogland and Lynn Bullard, botanists from CSIRO, stayed in Wagu while studying the unique Hunstein Range plants and collecting for the National Museum in Canberra. The Dyes were also hosts to Douglas Newton, an art collector from the Rockefeller primitive art museum and staff from the regional governor's office.

Hosting visitors and caring for four children took most of Sally's time. She wrote home about being frustrated that she could not do more with the language. Edie was in first grade that year and all the distractions kept her from getting her

The Dye family together in Wagu village in 1966

school work done. Wayne made real progress working with

Naba and Begai. Both men became good readers and were able to make real progress with language translation. They proved to be invaluable to Wayne and Sally in the development of the written language.

During this time, Edie wrote her first letter to her Grandma Edith. Edie and Joy were learning to swim, Tom was enjoying splashing in the shallow water and baby Jamey was just learning to thrive.

The Australian government proved to be very committed to the remote people of New Guinea. They spent significant resources on vaccines, medicine, and medical care. There was an unwritten rule that they would not go finding sick people, but if the people showed up at the hospital they would take care of them. They also worked closely with missionaries to supply medicine to the remote villages.

The previous year, one of Wafiyo's wives, Wana, had had a child born prematurely. Wayne and Sally had the mother and baby taken to Wewak for special care. The Wewak hospital took the baby and put her into an incubator. Wana returned to the village believing the baby had been stolen. Wayne and Sally had to work with the government to reunite the two in the spring of 1966. When little Jeni Niyabogo arrived in Wagu, Sally was there to teach Wana how to prepare simple foods that Jeni could eat, since her mother could not breastfeed her. Jeni thrived. The Wagu people were also learning to take their children to Ambunti if they needed medical attention in Wayne and Sally's absence.

Mifaha was a young toddler and the child of one of the men who was put in prison. She became very ill and passed out not long after Wayne and Sally had returned from Ambunti with little Jeni. The people said Mifaha was dead, but Sally rushed out to the fresh grave they were preparing to put Mifaha in. She could see Mifaha was in convulsions. She begged them to let her take Mifaha to the house and give medicine. She alerted Wayne. Amazingly, he was able to contact Ambunti hospital on their two-way radio. They told him to bring her in. He put together a rescue party and rushed Mifaha and her mother to Ambunti where she received an anti-malarial shot and recovered. They gave Wayne several vials of injectable quinine for use in similar cases in the village. Mifaha was completely well when they returned.

The following event is taken directly out of the Dyes' July 1966 prayer letter, written from Sally's perspective:

"Naintu is much worse," said Naba, our informant, as he stepped inside the door of our sago palm house. "He wants me to go across the lake in the morning to get his uncle so he can send away the kwonu and remove the bark they have put in his body. Can we rent your motor canoe?"

"I am sorry, Naba," Wayne answered using the simpler Gahom phrases that he had mastered. "I want to help Naintu, but I will not lend you the canoe. You cannot bring this man in my canoe."

Naba's shoulders dropped. His dark eyes pleaded. Wayne continued. "I will give Naintu a shot of penicillin. I gave him medicine for malaria first. It can give fever, chills, and headache this way."

Naba stepped back towards the door. "The shot will take care of his sickness," he mumbled, "but he will still die if we do not get rid of the kwonu.".

I spoke to Wayne. "We could go down and pray for Naintu. We can't just leave him like that. Of course, I'm sure God doesn't want us to condone the curing ceremony!"

"We'll come down and pray for Naintu," Wayne told the disappointed man.

Naba nodded without enthusiasm and went out into the night. For a few moments, Wayne and I discussed the situation and prayed for wisdom. Then we went out together, confident that God wanted to do something for these people.

We found Naintu lying by his fire with his wife Kaba sitting at his feet. Several people sat talking softly in the darkness, back in the far corner of the room. Sitting down quietly near Naintu, we prayed silently for direction. We sought only simplicity, for these people are so prone to look for ritual.

Wayne prayed first in our own language, and I did the same. I felt it necessary to command the spirit to leave in Jesus' name, as Paul did in Acts. Then the Holy Spirit gave Wayne facility in the Gahom language and he prayed, commanding the kwonu to leave in Jesus' name.

All voices in the room stilled in amazement. And quietly as we had come, we got up and left.

Next day when Wayne went to see Naintu and to give the first penicillin shot, he was moving about and feeling much better. He was convinced, without doubt, that God had sent the kwonu away and that they would not return. When Naintu's uncle did come, he, too, was amazed at what had taken place.

How our hearts rejoiced! God had shown Himself to the Gahom in a way they could understand!

This is just a beginning. May the Gahom people see their need for Jesus Christ as we translate God's Word for them."

All of these medical successes convinced the people that Sally was a powerful shaman. However, Wayne and Sally were seeing things differently. For them, the confrontation with Naintu was just another event in a string of events that started to convince them that they were facing more than just an ignorant people using superstition to explain the death that was around them. They had experienced the Ganbi night terrors, the timing of rain, the decision by the Wagu men to go kill a family in a neighboring tribe, and more. All these events and the circumstances around them caused Wayne and Sally to begin to believe that the Wagu people's behavior was being negatively influenced by listening to dark forces trying to keep them in bondage.

Other aspects of the culture also caused them to wonder about dark influences. The beliefs about women's monthly cycles being evil, the fact the pregnant women were banned from eating the very foods they needed most for their developing babies, the spousal and child abuse they witnessed -- all contributed to the conviction that the culture was corrupt and self-destructive and in need of transformation. Still Wayne and Sally struggled and did not want to be victims themselves of the superstitious thinking they saw around them.

During this time, Wayne experienced what he describes as an inner spiritual breakthrough. He felt assurance from God that despite his failures in language learning, in loving and knowing how to deal with the people, and even in getting along with Sally, he could take for himself the promise of John 15:16-17, "You did not choose me, but I chose you and appointed you so that you might go and bear fruit—fruit that will last—and so that whatever you ask in my name the Father will give you. This is my command: Love each other." He wrote this scripture verse out on his clipboard in permanent ink and would read it at the start of every work day.

Wayne and Sally returned to Ukarumpa in July, nervous to leave the babies but genuinely excited about what God was doing to show He was there for the people of Wagu. Throughout the spring and summer of 1966, they had been receiving special financial gifts that were earmarked for the construction of a new house at Ukarumpa. They had enough of the funds to get on the construction list, but were on the waiting list behind houses that were fully funded. The housing shortage at Ukarumpa was getting worse with the arrival of many new translators. The house builders were making a heroic effort to get as many houses built as possible before the November 1966 Branch Conference.

Their own house was started shortly before the conference. While under construction, the funds came in for materials almost on an as-needed basis. Money for the rainwater tank, the sink, and the septic tank all came just when they were needed for construction. When they moved into the house in November of 1966, it was not complete. It had the roof and floor, some interior walls, some cupboards and counters, but more work would need to be done after the conference. They were really happy to finally have their own place. There was fifty dollars left in the house fund when they moved in.

Wayne invited their good friend and Bible study leader, Al Pence, to perform the prayer at the new house dedication. Al was the new director. Before praying, Al gave a short speech. He said something in the speech that jumped out at Wayne and Sally independently and stuck with them the rest of their lives. "You have learned how to pray in faith and see God answer. Now ask God to show you something truly important to pray for."

After the dedication, they discussed the speech and both agreed that they should pray for converts in Wagu.

In reviewing the letters and documents for preparing this book, this prayer is a clear indication of a shift in understanding of prayer in the PNG Branch of Wycliffe. Early in their arrival at PNG, Wayne and Sally were frustrated by the Branch leadership's lack of conviction that God answered prayer in specific ways. Now this new director was admonishing them to pray for God's specific answers to prayer.

Chapter 14 – Striving and Thriving

Christmas of 1966 found Sally back in the Lae hospital with Jamey. He had contracted the measles, followed by malaria and pneumonia. A passenger had resuscitated Jamey when he stopped breathing on the flight to Lae, and the doctors were very concerned for his welfare. Wayne stayed at Ukarumpa with Edie, Joy, and Tom.

Wayne and Sally heard word from the village through the Farnsworths that the Wagu women had stopped giving their children anti-malarial medications and babies were dying again. Wayne and Sally were scheduled to return to Wagu in February of 1967 but were feeling a sense of foreboding over returning. All these things were weighing heavily on their minds:

•   The near death of Jamey in December was a recent memory, and Sally did not want to put him through the transition back to the Sepik.

•   The people had stopped listening and were returning to their old ways, and children and elders were dying because of it.

•   Wayne and Sally had not completed their linguistic work enough to start translating.

•   The Hunstein River was completely clogged with grass islands, making the trip eight hours of hard work through clouds of mosquitoes and hot sun.

•   They were faced with the prospect of leaving Edie in a boarding school (children's home) rather than returning with the family to Wagu.

Note: Care and education of missionary children is one of the more difficult and controversial subjects related to missions in general and pioneer missions in particular. There is an extended discussion of the children's home at the Wagu rainforest website www.wagurainforest.com\FromFeartoFreedom - The Book. In most modern missionary settings, children are homeschooled through sixth or seventh grade and sometimes even through high school. During the 1970s, homeschooling became integrated with the Ukarumpa school system so children could continue the same curriculum in the village and pick it up at Ukarumpa.

Sally wrote home, "We are actually thinking about giving up on the tribe. Others have. There are plenty of things for us to do on the base."

They did see their discouragement as hindering the advancement of their goal to establish a church in Wagu and asked for prayer. They were confident in the message they received from their director during their Ukarumpa house dedication. They needed to be in the village for God to use them in making that happen. However, facing the reality of returning to Wagu was overwhelming. They reached out to their friends Dick and Loretta Loving for advice and prayer. The Lovings embraced the idea of spiritual warfare and were more than willing to pray for God's power to overcome their discouragement. After prayerful consideration, they agreed to return to Wagu and began making plans to be in the village by early February.

While Sally prepared Edie for the children's home, Wayne returned to Wagu Village with supplies first and rallied help in cleaning up the house since they had been away over a year. Then he went back to Ambunti and picked up Sally, Joy, Tom, and Jamey from the Ambunti Guest House. The grass was bad in the Hunstein River, but the water was in flood stage and they were able to go and come through the Yambun cutoff.

While some babies had died while they were gone, more had been born. The number of children around the village was encouraging. By this time, the medical team at Ambunti were convinced that the primary cause of the deaths in Wagu was malaria. Wayne and Sally began to think through what practical changes they could make in the lives of the people to help protect them from this vicious disease.

The biggest concern upon arrival was the health of Naba. He had made it his personal responsibility to guard the house so when he got a tropical ulcer that threatened his life, he refused to leave the village to get medical help. Wayne and Sally arrived to find him very sick. He responded well to penicillin (the antibiotic of choice for most infections which was given by injection) and was soon recovering well.

The men were back from jail. Wafiyo had brought back with him a flyer on salvation written in Tok Pisin. He asked Wayne to translate it for him. The men of Wagu were eager to learn more about God's book. The village was growing from others coming in from surrounding villages wanting to know more about Wayne and Sally and their powerful medicine. Wayne and Sally were beginning to approach confrontation and obstacles as spiritual battles and starting to pray through situations before they took action.

Not long after they arrived, Naba told them about a man named Wadi in Yigai who was very sick and needed a doctor. Wadi had witnessed Wayne and Sally's powerful medicine back in 1964 and believed that it would help heal him, but he was too sick to make the trip to Ambunti or to Wagu. He sent word to Wagu requesting help. Wayne took Naba, Kiyawi, and a few other men and tried to make it to Yigai through the thick grass built up in the Hunstein River. After several hours in the hot sun, they had not gotten out of the mouth of the lake and finally gave up, discouraged. Wayne returned to Wagu but could not let go of the feeling that he should go rescue Wadi. Wayne and Sally prayed for God to make it possible if Wayne was to intervene. Early that evening, a very strong wind came and blew all night long. The next morning when they looked out at the entrance to the Hunstein River, they saw that all the islands were gone and the mouth of the lake was clear.

He and the men went down to Yigai with little resistance from the grass. They found Wadi unconscious with a badly infected and swollen leg. Wayne tried to take him so that he could get him to the Ambunti hospital, but Wadi's relatives refused to allow them. Instead, they threatened and argued with him. At first Wayne did not understand, and Naba explained to him that if Wadi died away from Gahom land, then his ghost would return and haunt them. Besides, he was too sick to be healed even by Wayne's powerful medicine. Wayne tried to reason with them but was not getting very far. The village was afraid of Wadi's sister who had threatened sorcery if they took away Wadi's body. Wayne was determined and finally asked them if he could pray a prayer of protection against the kwonu. He explained to them God was more powerful than the kwonu and that if he prayed, his God would protect them. They agreed to release Wadi on those terms. Wayne prayed for protection on the village and the crew in the canoe, and the village released Wadi to go with Wayne to Ambunti.

In Ambunti, Wadi underwent surgery to remove some of the infection and then was placed on antibiotics to finish the healing process. He eventually returned to Yigai, healed and grateful. For Naba and the other men who had helped Wayne take Wadi to Ambunti, this event was a powerful demonstration of God's power over both the wind and the kwonu of the Gahom people.

Meanwhile, Sally was trying to give the babies more protection from mosquito bites. She began to brainstorm ways to get babies sleeping in mosquito nets. Most adults build up some immunity to malaria over time, and the new babies get some boost from the colostrum in their mothers' milk. However, even healthy adults with a strong immune system will get sick if they are bitten too often, and the babies were especially vulnerable. In some parts of the Sepik, the native tribes had learned to make large hand-woven cocoons for sleeping, but the Wagu people had no such knowledge. They had not been needed inside the jungle of the Hunstein Range because it had little standing water and fewer mosquitoes than the Sepik marshlands. Wayne and Sally would conclude years later that moving to Wagu Lake was ultimately the largest cause of the extinction of the Genesowayagu language and the death of the people who spoke it.

Note: It has been argued by anthropologists that the mere presence of Western peoples in the Sepik River was a driver to bring the Genesowayagu people out of the jungle and to the lake, and that in turn was causing the extinction prior to actual contact with the West. It is speculated that many languages went extinct in the region without actual Western contact.

Wayne and Sally made several attempts to import mosquito nets but ran into two problems right away. First, the nets were much more comfortable so naturally the men took them, and the women and children were still left sleeping out in the open. Second, the Western style nets were both fragile and see-through. Since several couples lived in the same house, Wagus preferred opaque cloth nets to give privacy and warmth. The people had started to get clothes and wanted help mending them, and Sally wanted to teach them to mend the few mosquito nets they had, so she began teaching them to mend and eventually to sew. Sally also started working on supply sources to get them enough cloth that they could sew nets for the

Sally administering antibiotics

women and children.

The presence of new ideas and the power of the Western missionaries became a threat to the traditional beliefs of some of the tribal men. Wayne and Sally were first exposed to the antagonism between their belief system and the local religion in the nearby village of Yambun. Their friends, the Farnsworths, were farther along in their translation than Wayne and Sally. They were actively teaching people in the village to read the Bible in their native language. Apparently, this concerned a group of tribal priests who were practicing traditional Tamberan ancestor ceremonies. These men threatened those learning to read that if they did not stop, the men would perform sorcery and send the spirits of their ancestors to kill the ones learning to read or their family members. This tension would continue to grow and still exists today. There are many stories of power struggles between modern churches and traditional Tamberan religion all up and down the Sepik River.

There was also some practical wisdom that Wayne and Sally developed from experience. Initially, the people mainly asked for medicine for headaches. Wayne and Sally developed treatment strategies for dealing with the major deadly diseases in the village. The four most common killers of adults in the Sepik area at the time were infections from tropical ulcers, pneumonia, malaria, and tuberculosis. By 1967, Sally had developed a strategy that worked for three out of the four causes. Since the people had no shoes, the soles of their feet were like shoe leather. However, sharp stones and thorns would still cut right through and get infected. She learned to treat the wounds with salt water soaks and topical antibiotic creams for the infections. She would administer either oral or injected anti-malarial medication for the malaria. The government clinic provided injectable penicillin for the pneumonia and infected wounds.

This approach worked for most people most of the time, but not always. Sally had several cases where men had come from neighboring villages to be treated for an ulcer or infection. She would start them on a regimen of three to five penicillin injections, depending on the disease. As soon as they started feeling better, they would return to their village only having received a portion of the required antibiotic. The men would die days later because the penicillin had not completely killed the infection. This was extremely frustrating so she developed a technique where she would give the three days in one dose of penicillin. This was divided into two injections, one in each buttock. This was painful for several days, but seemed to work and would shock kill the infection. It became policy that in cases where Wayne and Sally treated people that were a "flight risk," they would resort to this technique.

Tuberculosis patients could only be treated in the coastal hospital in Wewak. No Wagus would go there and stay long enough for treatment. However, when their pneumonia and malaria were treated, they sometimes became strong enough to keep the TB from advancing.

A significant event occurred in the spring of 1967. Wayne and Sally had been specifically praying for converts since the Ukarumpa house dedication the previous November. Naba approached Wayne; he had read and understood Wafiyo's flyer and was ready for commitment of faith. Wayne prayed the prayer of salvation with him and he became the first Christian in Wagu from the Gahom people.

One evening Wafiyo's wife Faisowa urged her brother-in-law Minal up the stairs to the Dyes' house. He was carrying his convulsing six-year old son Bosai. His mother followed them, carrying his younger brother. Faisowa called out, "San Sally, a *kwonu* has hit Bosai. Minal wants to bury him. Can you give him the medicine that can bring him back to life?" Sally had known Bosai over the year his father had been in prison. His distinguishing mark was a folded ear lobe, probably damage from an infection a couple of years previous. He was unconscious but clearly still alive from a medical perspective. Sally directed them into the larger room. Minal resisted. "Bosai is dead. I am going to bury him. You don't realize how powerful these *kwonu* are. Your medicine cannot possibly help because the *kwonu* has already killed Bosai." Sally stood in front of the door, blocking his exit with Bosai still in his arms. "Bosai is not dead yet. God is stronger than the malaria *kwonu*," she insisted.

Sally was beginning to panic. Wayne had stayed overnight in Ambunti to meet the next day's plane. She did not have his backup. She could not prepare the medicine without some help to keep Minal from leaving with his son. "Help, Lord!" After that prayer, she thought of Naba. "Faisowa, please go get Naba to come and talk with Minal."

Naba came quickly. He was able to calm Minal and convinced him to put Bosai down by his wife and stay while Sally boiled the needle and syringe for the injectable anti-malaria. While it was boiling, she had to guess Bosai's weight because they had no scales. Then she filled the syringe, ready to give the injection, praying all the time that it would work. "Dear God, please help me to do the right thing. Help me save this little boy's life. Help me communicate your truth and your strength to these people."

Meanwhile, Bosai continued to have jerking convulsions, but they were not strong enough to cut off his airway. Every time he convulsed, his mother took up the ritual mourning, but quietly. She helped in positioning him for the injection while Sally gave it. Sally looked over at Naba. He had calmed Minal. Then, she asked Naba to pray in Bahinemo that God would save Bosai's life. He prayed fervently and wisely. Naba also helped prepare them for the long wait for the medicine to work. Minal paced the floor for a long time then instructed his wife and left the house.

Soon Bosai stopped convulsing and went to sleep. His mother continued to watch over him, dozing at times. It was around dawn that Bosai woke up and asked his mother for some food. She excitedly woke everyone. Within an hour, Bosai was able to stand and walk with his father's help. Minal commented, "It could not have been a *kwonu*. If it was, Bosai would have died."

Wayne and Sally had been wrestling with how to explain to the Wagu the nature of malaria and the power of medicine to overcome it. In the Bahinemo worldview, a mere physical disease could not kill; only a *kwonu* spirit could do that. So why use medicine to treat someone who was dying and so "must have been attacked by a *kwonu*?" Was it truthful to say medicine could kill *kwonu*? What would be the impact years later from this way of describing the process? What was the relationship between evil forces and physical illness anyway?

They were now sure of one thing; if they stayed with the strictly Western explanation they believed to be more truthful, it was sure to result in many deaths. In that moment of desperation with Minal, Sally had said Bosai had a "malaria *kwonu*." After discussion and prayer, they decided to keep speaking of the "malaria *kwonu*," which could be killed by medicine if taken in time. This explanation addressed one of the major roadblocks standing in the way of physical healing -- the difficulty of gaining permission to give medicine. From Sally's perspective, the fear and resistance to treatment did in fact feel like a form of spiritual oppression. Including the spiritual world in the conversation of physical healing was beginning to challenge Wayne and Sally's Western training in ways that surprised them and caused subtle changes in their own worldview.

Minal was trying to rally the Gahoms who had been in prison to go back with him to their home in Gahom village. The government had helped them to make peace with the Begabegis after the group raid and killing. As their leader, Minal knew he had to re-establish the village or their prime land would be taken over by the neighboring groups. However, several of the men from Gahom had been affected by all God had done in saving their children. They were talking about staying longer to hear more of God's message.

One evening the Dyes heard an unusual sound—*whap, whap, whap*—the sound of something flapping against the ground. Someone was calling out strong statements they could not hear clearly. Wayne went out to find out what was going on. He could see that Begawi was pounding the ground with the heavy end of a palm branch and making a pronouncement with each whap of the branch. Begawi was Mifaha's father. He had witnessed several people who were healed, and heard about others. Naba was standing at a distance, watching the ritual. He explained that Begawi was using this palm branch ritual to proclaim that he planned to stay in Wagu and hear more about Jesus. He dids not want to go back to Gahom. He was hoping to convince his young followers and their families to stay also. Many men did decide to stay, along with their wives, children and young men who looked up to them: Mifaki, Isekweli, Wani, Hebei, Kwofiya, Kyenwa, Yaba, Mufan and younger Taho stayed in Wagu. About fifteen stayed, almost half of the group from Gahom. Those who were to leave for Gahom waited until after Wayne and Sally left for Ukarumpa. Minal, Mawi, Taho, Bahofa and Yanowei then took their families back to Gahom.

Wayne collecting word list to determine language.

Not long after this, Wayne was asked to do another language survey with the Townsends in a part of the region where Dr. Schuster's research showed people speaking languages similar to Bahinemo. Sally returned to Ukarumpa with the children before they left. On this trip, the Townsends would travel down the Sepik River to the Karawari River, and up the Krosmeri and on up the Salumei River to the south side of the Hunstein Range. The Wagus had told stories of people groups in that area that had not been in contact with the West. The Townsends wanted to meet with them to better document how their cultures were being impacted by Western influences. Wycliffe was interested in learning about the languages in each region. Wayne would be able to make contact with some remote Bahinemo people. The trip would be funded in part by the Townsends' research grant.

Wayne took Naba, hoping to use some of the time to help him understand Christian faith. They took a houseboat along with Wayne's canoe. On the trip, they visited seventeen villages from fourteen language groups, including Menesuyo and Meli from Bahinemo. Linguists had developed a technique of collecting word lists to determine a language group. They had a preselected group of nouns that were easy to communicate like bird, fish, canoe, etc., and they would interact with a person or group of people to determine their word for that noun. They would then compare the words to established lists from other language groups to see how similar the two languages were. This turned out to be quite an adventurous trip on which Wayne pulled an arrow from a man's groin. They were able to radio the government, which came for him in a speedboat and took him to Wewak hospital. Wayne kept the arrow tip as a souvenir.

On this trip Wayne also discovered that he and Sally were having an impact on the whole language group and not just on Wagu village. The word about Wadi's healing had reached them and they knew about Wayne and Sally's God and his power over the *kwonu*. Wayne and Sally wrote home very encouraged and were determined to return and spend time with these remote people.

After the survey, Wayne returned to Ukarumpa. Jack Ruth had arrived at Ukarumpa as a new Wycliffe member with a civil engineering degree, thus relieving Wayne of some of the duties that kept him at Ukarumpa.

In May of 1967, Wayne and Sally prepared to return to Wagu to continue working on the translation. Two young single missionaries, Marilyn Laszlo and Pat Converse, were available for two weeks to help out. Marilyn would type and input data for them, and Pat would supervise Joy's home school. Marilyn was young, ambitious, and capable. She was interested in the Sepik area and this was an opportunity for her to get experience in village life in the Sepik. Wayne and Sally needed to return to Wagu in order to make sufficient progress in the language analyses to attend the July translation workshop. That would make it possible to translate some Scripture to leave in Wagu while they went on furlough.

Then they received a message from Robin in Yambun that the water level in the Sepik had dropped so low that the Yambun shortcut was no longer an option, and they were going to have to find a way through the grass-clogged Hunstein River. Wayne, Sally, Marilyn, and Pat flew to Ambunti anyway, thinking that the reports were overstated and that once in Ambunti they would figure out a solution. However, all those who had tried to navigate the Hunstein had failed, even in narrow paddle canoes. By Friday, the four of them grew deeply discouraged, fearing they would have to charter another flight and return to Ukarumpa, unable to do any work on the language.

They joined with Harry and Carole Box, who were also at the guest house on a trip to record several more Sepik languages. They prayed together as a group for God to show them some way to get to Wagu. With no other known option, Sally felt led to pray that God would clear the river of grass by Monday.

They sang a hymn of thanks. Then, as soon as they opened their eyes from the prayer, it began to rain.

It rained for two days and nights. The storm seemed to be localized in the Hunstein range, causing high currents coming down the Hunstein River. Wayne and Sally watched in amazement as floating islands started traveling past the guest house in Ambunti. "Where is this grass coming from?" they asked the locals. "From that river you go up to Wagu," was the response. Monday morning, the sun was shining. Wayne and several men loaded up the canoe with supplies and headed upriver to Wagu. The flooded Hunstein River had flushed out all of the grass. Wayne returned and took the ladies and children on Tuesday. They actually returned to Wagu with no delays. Wayne wrote home to his parents praising God for his providence and quoting the following scripture in the King James version, "*When he putteth forth his sheep, he goeth before them.*"

The Wagu people were amazed at the storm and did not recall that the grass had ever cleared after only one storm. Pat Townsend had been recording the rains for the two years she was in New Guinea and commented on the significant quantity and timing of the rain. We have no record of the magnitude of the storm or how much of an anomaly it really was for that season of the year. For those who had prayed and those in the local area who witnessed the event, there was no doubt that it was a strange occurrence with very precise timing and a significant positive impact.

In the following weeks, Wayne and Sally and their team completed the pre-translation jobs they were there to complete. Pat and Marilyn were a huge help, and the men were very eager to help with the translation. Wayne's ability in language was improving; he felt like the people were starting to understand the real power of the Gospel message.

One of the break-through memories from that summer's trip to Wagu occurred when Wayne was translating the list in Mark 7:22 of the evil actions that come out of a person's heart. He asked the Wagu men, "What did your ancestors tell you about these evil things?"

The men immediately agreed that the ancestors had told them all these actions were bad. When he asked them if any of them did these bad things, Begai spoke for all of them, "Definitely. Who could keep all of those rules? We are people of the ground." Wayne took that opportunity to explain that God was angry because they had not followed what they knew to be right. That is why He sent Jesus to pay the price for their failure. This was a key change in the Wagu people's understanding of the Bible as it relates to a holy God who is concerned about their personal behavior.

In Wayne's July report, he listed duck hunting, fishing, and swimming as recreation. They had found a small stream called Kakabu at the far end of the lake. The water was clear and cool, but shallow enough for the kids to play in. It also had some still pools that might be six feet deep in places. They would take the motor canoe over to escape the heat and chaos of the village. They also went back to the upper Hunstein for a family camping trip to finish out the last week before returning to Ukarumpa the end of August. The New Guinea branch had formed an anthropology committee to discuss techniques and address cross-cultural communication and issues, and Wayne was asked to help teach it.

In general, 1967 was a very positive year where they saw God working in powerful ways in Wagu village. They were progressing on the translation, they had their first convert, several men learned to read in Sally's trial literacy class, they were learning to relax and enjoy the village, the people were trusting them and following their medical guidance, and they were making progress in teaching the Bible.

For the Wagu people, there was a new mood of real hope. After seeing people healed when they thought death was inevitable, they were beginning to believe that it was possible to have power over death and the demons that haunted their world. This was not the kind of excitement they had felt when they started using Western tools; this was deeper -- a genuine hope that it was possible to overcome the power of the *kwonu* with the power of God.

Back at Ukarumpa, Wayne was happy to have another civil engineer to hand over the responsibility for surveying, water, and other projects requiring professional background. Jack Ruth was smart, creative, and hard-working. He did not plan to be a field translator but wanted to stay at Ukarumpa. He took over most of the remaining engineering projects which freed Wayne up to focus on the language. Another nice change was that Ukarumpa now had a large central generator that produced enough electricity to run the whole base.

Wayne and Sally received a special gift to have their house wired, but they chose to go without electricity until after furlough in order to replace their broken camera. The Skinners were leaving for furlough and offered to sell them theirs. Wayne and Sally were thinking ahead about their return to the US to visit family in less than a year. They would be reporting to the churches what God was doing, and hoped to get photos to help explain their living situation and work.

Daryl Lancaster had come to New Guinea to become the store manager. He could see the need for a larger variety of food and modern equipment for all the new houses being built. He and his family improved the lifestyle of everyone significantly. He also had a vision for training local nationals to take over much of the future responsibility for the store.

There was more evidence in the official Branch literature that showed a shift in the culture at Ukarumpa related to their views on prayer and spiritual warfare. Gladys Strange had come down with a bad case of hepatitis that was complicated by pneumonia and malaria. She was very ill. Before sending her on the plane to a regional hospital, the leaders anointed her with oil and laid hands on her in prayer. She recovered fully within a few weeks. While Wayne and Sally were not involved in the prayer meeting, these changes in corporate culture were aligning well with their own changes in approaching God in prayer. The New Guinea Branch senior leadership was actively seeking God's hand for healing.

Money was still tight, and they were often in the red at the end of the month, but Wayne and Sally were learning to thrive in both Ukarumpa and in Wagu.

Chapter 15 The Birth of the Wagu Church

Wayne and Sally returned to Wagu with the children in December 1967 to discover that the Wagu men had built a literacy building so they could hold larger literacy classes and more could learn to read. Naba and Begai may have had in mind meeting place for a possible future church, having seen

Teaching reading.

structures like that in their travels. The building held around fifty people and was designed like the village houses, only without the elevated bark floor. They had cut up old canoes as benches and had windows to let in the light and the breeze. This was the first time the Wagu people had taken the initiative on a church related project without Wayne and Sally's prompting, a very encouraging sign.

Sally started both beginning and advanced literacy classes soon after they arrived. She created a series of primers, introducing a few letters at a time in a syllable method. Sally copied most of primer pages on poster paper so all could see them at once. Wayne ordered larger plywood and blackboard paint to facilitate the reading and writing.

That Christmas, Wayne and Sally hosted Victor and Nonnie Barnes, whose two children were similar in age to Joy and Edie. Vic and Nonnie were medical officers in Ambunti and did not want to expose their children to the intense drinking that was typical of government employees at Christmastime in the East Sepik. They had a very traditional Christmas, complete with Christmas tree and presents (thanks to gifts sent by Sally's parents, Val and Curly Folger).

The Wagu people heard the Christmas story for the first time in their own language. Sally would later describe this as rather strange and lacking in meaning to them, especially since they had no context with which to understand the story.

After the Barnes returned to Ambunti, Wayne and Sally needed a break and decided to take a few days camping before Edie and Joy returned to school. Wayne had had quite a bit of success running upriver in the canoe, so they decided to try going up the Hunstein to find a place to camp. What they did not know is that the Hunstein upriver from Wagu consists of a very long winding section through the Sepik lowland swamp before it turns south into the mountains. It is a beautiful boat trip through forest with great wildlife, but there really is no good place to camp. Near sunset, they settled on a high bank in a large slow bend and set up camp as best they could. There was a sand bar for the kids to play on. Naba and Begai helped them set up the kitchen.

They made the best of it, in spite of the night's mosquitoes and chiggers, but it was not the break they were desperately hoping for. In the afternoon of the second day, Begai pulled Wayne aside and whispered to him.

"Do you really want your children playing so close to a mother crocodile guarding her nest?" Wayne was horrified! "What do you mean, and why didn't you tell me?" "I thought you knew," Begai replied. They packed up and headed back to the village.

Several other such events happened in succession: Edie had a stomach virus that presented itself like an appendicitis attack; they rushed her to Ambunti. Tom and Jamey had bouts of malaria and tropical ulcers (the same kind that had made Wayne very sick in 1964), then a pet duck a Yambun man had given the children was eaten by a large python.

The last straw for Sally was when Nansuai brought her sick baby to Sally hoping she could save it. She lived in a camp Begawi had set up for his followers at the far end of the lake. Nansuai's baby died on the way. Sally tried to give it mouth-to-mouth resuscitation but was unsuccessful. She was overwhelmed with a sense of failure, feeling that her medical skills were not up to the task before her.

Sally cried most of that night out of a deep sense of failure. She had not become the perfect missionary she had expected to be from hearing about missionaries back home. She saw herself as impatient with her children and even with Wayne. Her language skills were inadequate. "Oh, God," she cried. "I've failed. I can't do this. Help me."

The next morning when Naba arrived to work on the literacy materials, she told him why she was upset. She said, "I am not able to do this job anymore. I want to go home to my parents and family." Naba was shocked. "You can't leave now. Wayne is finally learning the language well enough to tell us what God is saying. We are beginning to understand; it is making sense." Naba responded, without Wayne and Sally's knowledge, by calling as many villagers as he could convince together to pray for Wayne and Sally, asking that they would be encouraged and stay and finish what they had started. This was the first time a group of Bahinemo people had ever gathered together to pray.

Wayne wanted to encourage Sally as well. He searched for Bible promises that might help her. He wrote them out on cards and pinned them on the bedroom wall where she could not miss seeing them. As she read them, one drew her attention: 1 Peter 5:8-10. It would get her through the next month.

"Be self-controlled and alert. Your enemy the devil prowls around like a roaring lion looking for someone to devour. Resist him, standing firm in the faith, because you know that your brothers throughout the world are undergoing the same kind of sufferings. And the God of all grace, who called you to his eternal glory in Christ, after you have suffered a little while He will himself restore you and make you strong, firm and steadfast."

Sally's faith, joy, and resolve returned.

Sally worked with Wayne, modifying the suggested scripts Gospel Recordings had sent them, then Wayne and his Wagu team translated them into Bahinemo. Sally returned to Ukarumpa with Jamey and the girls to settle Joy and Edie into a children's home while Wayne stayed on with Tom in the village. This was a much-needed break from the village and allowed Sally some time to grieve and heal. At the beginning of those weeks in Ukarumpa, she wrote a prayer letter documenting the events of January 1968. The letter was so depressing that the person who mailed their letters refused to mail it. Sally returned a few weeks later with improved spirit.

Meanwhile, back at the village Wayne was making real progress on the translation and in discussing the meaning with the men. Begai became the second convert and the first man in a leadership position to follow Christ. The translation sessions began to morph into Bible studies.

Also during this time, Harry Box, the recording specialist, spent days recording the passages developed by Wayne and a team of local language translators. Each short sermon took hours to record. Wayne read each phrase, then the Bahinemo repeated it a couple of times. When the words and intonation sounded right, he read it into the microphone. Any mistakes were erased by manually backing up the tape, and the phrase was repeated until it was correct. Harry then carefully spliced together the recorded phrases into a smooth sounding tape and duplicated it. It would take months for them to be edited, records pressed, and the records shipped back to Ambunti.

The plan was for Wayne and Sally to distribute the hand-crank record players to Wagu and the remote Bahinemo villages. The records were designed to be a clear articulation of the gospel message and the path to salvation for people who could not read. Harry gave Wayne a copy of his master tape, and Wayne also kept a paper copy of what they recorded, so they did not need to wait for the records to be returned.

Each evening the people of Wagu gathered in the literacy building and listened intently as he read or played it. Begai and Naba answered questions. More people, including Kokomo, joined the Wagu Sunday Bible studies led by Begai. Wafiyo was the next leader who made a profession of faith in Christ in these meetings.

After the Boxes left mid-February, Wayne and Sally loaded up the motor canoe and headed down river to follow the route Wayne had taken with the Townsends to the far side of the language group. He wanted to visit the Wefei and Menesuyo villages and read them the story scripts. Naba and Wafiyo came with them and witnessed to the people in their own language, then Wayne read the scripts to them.

In Menesuyo, there was a lot of interest in the gospel message. However, in Wefei village, Wayne took several genealogies but not that of the leader, thinking he did not want to bother him with all that tedious, detailed questioning. Wayne didn't realize how important genealogies were to establishing relationships and therefore to reinforcing the social structure. By not asking the leader first, he had been subtly undermining the man's authority.

That evening, when they had gathered again to hear the gospel recordings, the leader deliberately lay down and pretended to sleep. Wayne thought he was just tired, but Wafiyo and Naba knew immediately that the Dyes and their message had been rejected. Wafiyo and Naba excused themselves politely and picked up Tom and Jamey to get them safely back to their shelter. They told Wayne that they had better leave as soon as possible or risk getting hurt. The river was in flood and too dangerous to go that night, but Naba and Wafiyo kept alert and awakened Wayne and Sally before dawn. Sally dressed the children, and Wayne packed while Naba and Wafiyo loaded the canoe. They took off as soon as they could see to avoid snags in the rushing river

On the long canoe ride back to Wagu, Wayne wrote a twelve-page letter to his brother Gordon. He told Gordon that they ran the outboard motor for thirty-eight hours, round trip. The trip from Wagu to Menesuyo had involved traveling down the

Bowi making clothes with a foot peddle sewing machine.

Hunstein River to the Sepik River, then downriver to the Karawari River, the upriver to the Krosmeri, then upriver to the Salumei and way up past many snags and rapids to the south side of the Hunstein range.

When Wayne and Sally returned to Wagu, they again played the tapes, and discovered that the Wagu people had become eager to hear more of the gospel. They had seen God repeatedly help Wayne and Sally in their weakness, and concluded that He might help them as well. They listened to the recorded sermons nearly every day with growing understanding. Sally brought sewing supplies, and material for making clothes and mosquito nets by hand. Sewing machines were not yet available. That spring of 1968, Sally spent a lot of time teaching the women to sew and repair their own clothes.

Wayne pushed hard on translation every day. They sent to the printers in Ukarumpa four books that would be printed and sent back to Wagu before the Baptism in July 1968. The first book *Bili Tekoful* "What Happened First," was Genesis 1 through 9 and Exodus 20. The second was *God Tata Demomo* "What God Said," 30 key verses from Matthew and Ephesians. The third was *Jisas Tata Disiyam* "How Jesus Died," Mark 14-16. The fourth was about how the Jews lived, explaining some Jew-

Begai leads a Bible study

ish cultural customs. That is all the Dyes could leave in the language before they went on furlough.

During this time Edie and Joy were having a miserable time in the children's home. Edie was a fairly good writer by fourth grade and she cited a number examples of strict and abusive behaviors in the children's home. Edie most often wrote about the mistreatment of Joy rather than herself. By nature, Edie was very submissive compared to Joy, so it was highly likely that the bulk of the confrontations were directed at Joy. Most of the stories centered around severe punishments for relatively minor infractions. Some of these were related to culturally different parenting styles between Americans and Australians.

Tom was out in the village learning to canoe, hunt, and fish. Wayne wrote that Tom was able to paddle a dugout canoe by himself. (Wayne added "with a life jacket" for his mother's sake). Jamey was still too young to spend too much time away from his mother, but he spent a lot of time with Kereniyo, the family house helper. By now, Sally had relaxed and allowed the boys to have a freer rein with other people in the village.

At the end of March, they flew to Ukarumpa for a special literacy course and an anthropology workshop[1]. Edie and Joy were ecstatic to be out of the children's home. Sally prepared the translated books for printing, and the family took a few days' vacation in Goroka. By mid-June, they were back in Wagu. Wayne and Sally had written a letter to the director requesting a delay in their return to Michigan for furlough. They wanted more time to nurture the new Wagu Church. They were denied the request so proceeded to schedule their return for August 1968. In order to make as much progress as possible before leaving, they asked Judy Rehberg to came out to help Sally teach more people to read. Marilyn Laszlo also came during part of that time to help Wayne prepare more books.

By late June, there were more and more converts in Wagu. Begai and Naba were leading Sunday Bible Studies. They asked Sally to teach them some of the Tok Pisin hymns they had heard at Ukarumpa. Sally was aware that the hymns sung in church were a very different style of music with different notes from their music. The Bahinemos who had not been out of their area would find it very difficult to sing them. Sally wanted to encourage them to use their own musical style.

She had spent some time learning about the new study of indigenous music referred to as "ethnomusicology" from Dr. Vida Chenoweth who was also translating in the PNG highlands. Sally had begun to analyze the various Bahinemo genres:

---

their work songs and the bamboo pipe music sung "by the *wulyal* spirits." Each animal, plant, and ground formation was created by a different *wulyal*; each had a different song with its dance. She also discovered that most of these songs were not in their language at all. They would exchange goods with other groups for songs they saw as particularly successful. They knew which part of creation the song was sung for, but not the words. Sally gave up trying to use the analysis to create songs for them.

One day after a Sunday Bible study, Naba asked again for songs to sing. Sally replied, "Call some people together who want songs to praise God. Pray together and ask God to give you a song to praise Him." A few hours later, they came back to Wayne and Sally and excitedly sang the song God gave them. It was in good Bahinemo style. "*Jesus nakani tata deba. Nuwata nuwata, nuwata nuwata, tata deba.*" (Jesus is my brother, like that. Day after day, day after day, like that.) Over the next month, they created twenty-three songs to sing during the Bible studies which were gradually turning into worship services led by Begai with Naba assisting and Yafei giving summary confirmations normal for leaders.

During that time, Edie and Joy were staying with another translator couple, the Parringtons. The tone of Edie's letters from the time with the Parringtons was much more positive. She talked mostly about her pet turtle and guinea pigs.

In July 1968, the Dyes planned a baptism for all the new converts after they were carefully questioned regarding their faith. The baptism was administered by another local national pastor named Buria from Washkuk, the language group the Kooyers were working in. Fifty new believers were baptized in the stream at Kakabu. The whole village gathered there and sang the new Bahinemo praise songs from a printed four-page song book.

When Wayne and Sally sent their final prayer letter home in August of 1968, it was a story of hope and victory. They wrote about the transformation of the lives of the Wagu people from fear and anger to joy and peace. Here is a clip from the letter:

"Fifty Gahoms have accepted Christ! Men, women, and children have turned from their sin to live for Him. We have seen God work. We will never be the same again. Most amazing to us is the change in their lives and the joy on their faces.

Begai (bug eye), the threatening, strong-willed village leader, has become a thoughtful translation helper and responsible shepherd of the young church.

Wafiyo(wa fee yo), a wily, soft-spoken leader who could never be trusted, now loves the Lord and has won many of the others to Christ. He is burdened for the other villages around without Christ.

Kiyawi (key 'a we) used to be belligerent and lorded over everyone. Now this radiant young man speaks to God in a personal heartwarming conversation. He is gentle with others and is proving to be an apt teacher.

Bagi (ba 'gee) was the accepted leader when we came. He killed a man two years ago in a raid. He stole from everyone, a slave to his meager possessions. Now he has the peace that only God can give as he looks to a future reward in heaven.

Yafei ('ya fey) was the village curer. He interceded with the ghosts of the dead to heal disease and exorcise evil spirits. Now he has completely rejected his spirit contacts and is wholeheartedly living for Christ.

Wamini ('wa money) lived in constant fear of the spirits. Now he trusts the Lord for his protection and does all he can to help others."

195

Another young man who came to a place of faith in the Western God at this time was young Kokomo, the peace child between Nikilu and Kakilu.

In the six months between January 1968 and August 1968, the world had completely changed for Wayne and Sally. After four years of struggle and striving, they finally had hope. In January 1968, they were completely discouraged, ready to quit; in August, they were excited. In January, they were convinced that the village was not safe for their children; in August, they did not want to leave. In January, they had given up hope; in August, they were full of hope because of the birth of a new church full of believers who were excited about a life without fear of the spirits. This rapid and profound change began in January when Naba convinced his unbelieving friends to have a prayer meeting for these poor crazy white people who had come to the village to bring them a book.

Wamini was one of those new believers whose life had changed so dramatically after his conversion that everyone in the village saw the power of God to transform a man. He became loving and helpful to everyone. He was full of excitement and hope. The whole village was amazed at the change in his life.

Wamini made an appeal to the village elders and the church to move the village to a location across the lake. The location had firm beaches instead of mud, the high ground was more level, and there were several springs. The Wagu people had previously avoided it because of the fear of the spirits. They had seen strange clay objects there. A man who planted a garden there died. Yet, Wamini argued that now that they were children of God, they did not need to fear the spirits and should live on the better land. The village agreed and began the move to the new location.

The abrupt turnaround in Wagu reinforced a belief that Wayne and Sally had held since college: how one did pioneer missions was very important. Their experience with the Wagu people began to elevate in their minds the importance of anthropology-- how it could influence reaching remote people with the gospel. When they left to return to Michigan in September of 1968, they were both hopeful and nervous about the young Wagu church.

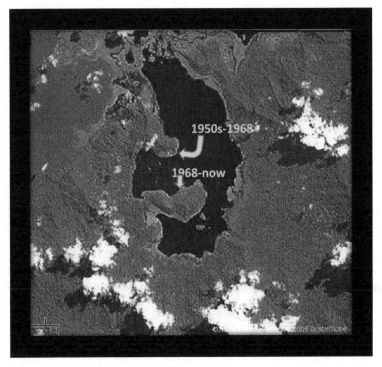

1950s-1968

1968-now

New and old location for Wagu Village

In November, with Wayne and Sally far away in America, Wamini became ill and died. Kiyawi immediately wrote them a letter:

"Wamini died. We are so sorry. Why did this happen? We are worried about him. He is young. Why? I am worried about the talk about his death. The people are listening to Satan. Now they don't want to hear

197

God's talk. This is not good, so I am writing to you."

However, after he wrote this, the church members became aware of something new. They remembered at the time of Wamini's death, there had been a lightning strike in the village. Strangely, no one was afraid around Wamini's body. They reasoned that his *dafa* spirit must have already departed. It would not remain to haunt them. Surely these things indicated this new teaching was true. Reassured, they resumed housebuilding at the new site.

Not long after this, the church began sending out preachers to other parts of the language group.

Young Kokomo became enthusiastic about his faith and was one of the first evangelistic pastors from the new church. He returned to his mother's village on the April River to witness to all he had seen and heard. While there, a porch roof caught fire and would have spread to the whole house, but Kokomo commanded the fire to stop in Jesus name. Two Bitara families returned with him to Wagu a few months later to hear more of the Good News. One of the children was Wadebu, a two-year old girl with clubbed feet. They hoped Jesus would heal her.

Naba returned to his childhood village of Yigai and Namu to tell them about Jesus and the core of the Gospel. Begai was reading and teaching in Wagu using the Tok Pisin New Testament and translating it for those who did not understand Tok Pisin.

The village had grown significantly; leadership grew with it. Yafei had significant power as a church leader, but there were other leaders as well.

The village leadership planned the new village together. They identified bathing areas for men and women, two springs upstream for water supply, locations for latrines, and a central no-build zone up the middle of the village. They negotiated individual lot locations for different families and grouped those houses around language groups.

Chapter 16 Furlough

By 1968, the price of trans-pacific airline flights was equivalent to ship transportation and took days instead of weeks. Wayne and Sally booked tickets through the Philippines and stopped several days visiting friends in Tokyo before returning to Michigan through Chicago. The Dyes arrived in Chicago in September of 1968. They were exhausted but glad to be back in the United States. Sally's sister Sandy lived near Chicago and put them up for the night.

Wayne and Sally were returning to Michigan after five years in New Guinea. Wayne had been accepted in the University of Michigan in Ann Arbor to finally finish his Master's degree in anthropology. Finances were tight. They were grateful when Grace Bible Church offered them the free use of an older three-bedroom house on a property the church had bought to build a new church. A friend offered an older station wagon for their use. Church members offered furniture and household items. Wayne started classes immediately while Sally organized the house and settled the children in school.

When they received Kiyawi's despondent letter about Wamini's death, Wayne and Sally were afraid for the church in Wagu. They asked their supporting churches to pray, and wrote encouraging letters to the Wagu church leaders. They also asked Neal and Martha Kooyers to visit the village and check on the church. In January, they received a very positive report containing the following statement:

"They [the Wagu church] are eager to learn the Bible and are meeting and worshiping three times a week. They are reading scripture and translating the Pidgin (Tok Pisin) *New Testament to gain more understanding. You don't need to worry about the church growing in Wagu."*

The Dyes visited friends and reported what God had done in Wagu to the churches that supported them that first term. The supporting churches at that time were Grace Bible Church of Ann Arbor, MI; Strathmoor-Judson Baptist Church, later a church plant Farmington Hills Baptist, and members of Sally's home church First Evangelical United Brethren of Battle Creek. Wayne and Sally were encouraged by the number of individuals in these churches who had become loyal supporters. Their members had been praying and sending money in spite of the limited information they had received.

The children were overwhelmed by so much change and meeting so many people. The family was given multiple Thanksgiving dinners and several Christmas celebrations in the homes of two different grandparents and aunts and uncles. All of the physical demands of these meetings took its toll on the four children and on Sally's back. Again she struggled with back pain.

Dr. Harry McIntosh, InterVarsity friend and loyal supporter, invited Wayne and Sally to interdenominational worship services that were open to dreams, healing, and personal relationships with God. After a meeting, Wayne and Sally invited a leader in the new movement, Graham Pulkingham, an Anglican priest, over to their home for coffee to hear more. While Sally was serving the coffee, Graham asked her, "Would you like to have me pray for your back?" She was surprised as she had not said anything about her back pain. She consented. Graham prayed a simple prayer for healing and then left. Sally's pain was gone and never returned.

Wayne and Sally hoped to leave for PNG in August after Wayne graduated in June with a Masters in Anthropology. Sadly, they did not have the pledges of funds Wycliffe required for their support, nor did they have enough to buy plane tickets. Again, they were facing the financial realities of depending on others for the resources to do what they believed God wanted from them. One longtime friend advised them to stay in Michigan, work and earn the money they needed. They considered her advice and prayed.

After prayer, Wayne did the math. He realized that it would take most of the income he would earn to support a family; it would take years to save up enough money to finance the return to New Guinea. They agreed together to pray something like this:

"Dear God, help. There is no way we can earn or raise the funds needed to go back to Wagu. If You want us there, You will have to arrange it and give us the faith to believe You can."

They both had a growing sense that God wanted them back in PNG and that He would provide the partners needed to keep them there. They were to set the date, give the reports where they were invited, and prepare to go.

Former InterVarsity members had settled in various communities in the area. When these friends heard their news and their need, they invited the Dyes to their churches to give reports. It was becoming clear to Wayne and Sally that the social network they had formed at InterVarsity was a core group which promoted their work in their churches. Family members and people who had changed churches also recommended them. Some of these listened and gave honorariums; others committed to annual support. They made initial contacts with three more churches that remain core supporting partnerships to this day: Highland Park Baptist Church in Southfield, Ward Presbyterian Church, now in Northville, and Immanuel Baptist Church of Saginaw, Immanuel Bible Church, founded by Wayne's martyred uncle, Cecil Dye.

These six and several other churches and a number of generous and faithful individuals made up a core support group that enabled them to work much more effectively through the rest of their careers. There were other honorariums, gifts, and support pledges that brought in enough funds for Wayne and Sally to return to New Guinea.

The Dyes were able to pack several key items in their crate, including:

- A gasoline-powered Maytag wringer clothes washing machine, donated by Grace Bible Church

- An old 1 ¼ horse outboard gas trolling motor for the children to use on the lake, given by Sally's father

- A Singer treadle sewing machine for the Wagu women, and

- An old gas stove with cast iron burners that did not rust in the humidity, both donated by a single mother.

These made a significant improvement in the quality of their lives in Wagu.

Taken in the 1970 this picture shows Jamey, Tom, and Edie enjoyin the Elgin outboard brought back in 1969.

Chapter 17 – Wagu Transformation

The Dyes arrived in Ukarumpa September 1st and met Naba and his new teenage wife Binuwei at Ukarumpa on September 2nd. Ukarumpa was a bit of shock for Binuwei. Wayne returned to Ambunti with Naba and Binuwei within 10 days, while Sally settled back into their house and enrolled Edie, Joy and Tom in the local mission primary school.

They did not know what to expect when they returned to Wagu, so the plan was for Sally to stay at Ukarumpa while

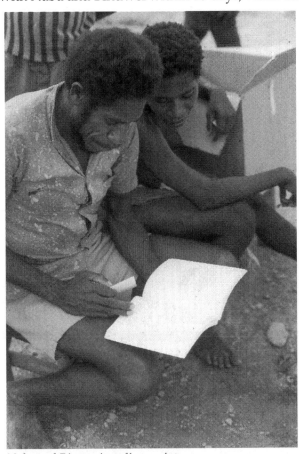

Naba and Binuwei reading scriptures.

Wayne returned to the village and investigated the situation. Naba had reported that the village had moved to the new site, which would require Wayne and Sally to build a new house.

Before leaving for Wagu, Wayne made a request of the building

207

department for his friend Bill Groot, a master carpenter, to join him in building the new house. The head of the building department said Bill was too busy building houses in Ukarumpa and would not be able to help. Wayne and Sally were disappointed, but still believed that Bill was the right person to help them. Right before Wayne left for the village they prayed, "Lord, if you want us to get carpenter help, you will have to change their minds or show us another way to get the house built [because we can't do it on our own]."

When Wayne arrived in Ambunti, several men from Wagu were there but his motor and canoe were not. However, he was eager to get to Wagu so he borrowed Neal Kooyers' canoe and found an outboard in Neal's repair shop to use. He loaded the canoe and headed to Wagu with Naba, Binuwei, and the men who were already in Ambunti. He made it as far as Yigai before the motor broke down and he had to spend the night. He had intended to use the nets from the old house, so he had to borrow a mosquito net from one of the Yigai villagers for the night. The next day he limped back to Ambunti with the motor running on one cylinder.

He came down with the flu and took a few days to recover and repair the motor with Neal's help.

Wayne finally made it to Wagu three days later, only to discover the village was mostly empty, as many of the men were out searching for food. The villagers that were there put him up in the new *haus kiap*, and he salvaged cooking supplies and sleeping equipment from the old house. The site of the decaying church building and the old village site was discouraging, and it felt to him at that moment that he was starting over.

When the men returned from gathering food, Wayne began discussing with the village leaders about potential locations for the new house. His adopted brother Wafiyo had reserved a space for him at the top of the village, but Wayne wanted to be near the lake for the view as well as the logistical advantages associated with access to the boat. The site he really wanted had been taken by Keniyofo, and so Wayne offered to pay him to move his house so they could have the site. Keniyofo accepted the funds and immediately began moving his house.

Wayne knew he needed building materials, and began to commission poles to be cut for specific columns and beams by size and type of wood. As each pole came in he would write the name of the person who brought it in order to pay them if he used that pole. These written names remained visible after the house was built.

He intended to make a portion of the house on a concrete slab foundation. This required a quantity of gravel to make the concrete so Wayne commissioned men to bring gravel from the local streams. He needed buckets and shovels from the old house to use in harvesting the gravel so he returned to the old village to collect materials for the project. The trip would also allow him to retrieve needed medical supplies from the old house to treat the constant stream of wounds and illnesses the villagers brought to him.

Discouraged by the need to start again and wandering through the old house, he discovered—still pinned to the wall—the verses he had put there to encourage Sally in her low point in January of 1968. The memories of the hardships of the previous five years came rushing back and he was overwhelmed with emotion. The misery of the first three weeks; the ever-present mosquitoes, the dog bite, centipedes, lack of water, living on canned food, hauling the children's bathroom waste in a can to the outhouse. He cried for a long time, grieving over the hard-

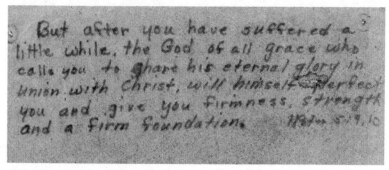

The note that led to Wayne's moment of introspection change

ship he had put Sally and kids through. Wayne had been raised to never cry, and he had no memory of crying as an adult, so the tears themselves were a new experience. Wayne read the passage on the wall from 1 Peter 5:9-10:

"And the God of all grace, who called you to his eternal glory in Christ, after you have suffered a little while He will himself restore you and make you strong, firm and steadfast."

These verses renewed his resolve, and he decided to do better with this new house. He returned to Wagu with an expanded vision and new drive to build a better house.

Wayne and Sally had already planned for a more permanent house this time, one that would last the rest of their time in Wagu and would meet their needs as well as the needs of the people. The new house would have space for a medical room, a new mother's birthing room away from the mosquitos, a kitchen and pantry, a small workbench and tool room, two bedrooms, a large loft for guests, and expansion of the plumbing into the bathroom. The general concepts Wayne designed into the first house were expanded on and perfected to minimize the mosquitos, maximize lake views, maximize capture of the cool(ish) breeze that came off the lake in the morning and evening, and be divided into bedroom spaces and public spaces for interaction with the village.

Towards the end of the first visit, while Wayne and the men were working on the house, Begawi came, urgently carrying Mifaha, his unconscious eight-year old daughter. She was still breathing, but as far as the village culture was concerned, she was already dead. By now, Wayne and Sally had fully embraced the idea that all unconscious victims should be treated with injectable quinine because the symptoms were nearly always caused by malaria. Wayne had written down the dosage for an adult, but found his notes too brief to provide a sure guide. He knew that without the injection, she would die, and he knew if he gave her too much, it could also cause her death. He guessed at the dosage and gave her the shot. Mifaha did come out of the coma but was deaf. While ecstatic that she was alive, Wayne worried that he may have under-dosed her. It was finally possible to radio the Ukarumpa doctor, who confirmed that cerebral malaria in her system had caused the deafness. The doctor told Wayne the sad news; deafness from this cause was incurable. The village elders asked Wayne to pray with them for the healing of her deafness, and he agreed, but qualified his prayer, saying God sometime chooses not to heal. There were no signs after the prayer of any healing.

The village got behind the new housing project and brought materials in quickly. Wayne made several trips back to Ambunti, picking up bags of cement and other supplies. Before his return to Ukarumpa, Wayne heard the positive news over the radio that the construction leader had changed his mind. Bill Groot would be allowed to help Wayne with the house. By the time Wayne returned to Ukarumpa a few weeks later, he had the foundation poured and the rest of the materials ordered to complete the project when he returned.

Wayne arrived back at Ukarumpa in early October to lead a two-week anthropology workshop. The PNG Branch now considered these workshops essential for new translators to better understand the culture and communicate more effectively from the beginning of their translation programs. After the workshop, Wayne and Bill were ready to go back to Wagu in November to start building the house.

Author's Note: Several years later, the Dyes were in a Bible study on the center with the head of the building department who had changed his mind about Bill Groot. They were discussing "getting guidance from God." Wayne asked him, "Remember when we needed to have Bill Groot go out to help us build our house? What made you change your mind?" He answered, "I never understood why, but I had a growing impression that I should let Bill go out and help you build it." For Wayne, this exchange served as confirmation that God was guiding others in answer to his prayers.

When Wayne returned to Wagu with Bill to work on the house, he asked how Mifaha was faring. They replied that she was doing fine. Then he asked, "How is she handling being deaf?" They casually replied, "Oh, she is not deaf. After you left we prayed again." Wayne pondered this and decided that their faith was stronger than his.

Wayne and Bill used longer-lasting Western materials, including a galvanized iron roof to collect rainwater. They had also planned for a larger water tank so the Dyes could make it through several months without rain, but, due to a shortage of funds, they settled on re-using the three 55-gallon drums from their first village house. These were the drums they had originally brought their goods in from the US in 1963.

On one of their trips to Ambunti, they stopped by Yigai. Naba reported that some kind of sickness had killed many people there, and now people were getting sick in Wagu as well. Wayne checked with the clinic in Ambunti and learned that the worldwide Hong Kong flu epidemic had struck this isolated area and was killing a large number of people. Ten percent of the people in Yigai had already died. Wayne knew he needed Sally's help if he was going to keep more people from dying. He called Sally on the radio and asked her to come help nurse the people and avoid more deaths. Even though the house was not finished yet, she was needed as soon as possible. Sally knew she could not bring the children out because of the flu. She even dreaded going herself.

The thought of returning to Wagu before the house was screened in brought flashbacks of the pain they had experienced building the first house: the humid heat, the mosquitoes, the pouring rain. Before the radio call, Sally had been reading C. S. Lewis' story about an imaginary trip to a place between heaven and earth guided by angels. In the story, a man had a lizard on his shoulder that kept telling him how much he needed it. The angel who came to help this man told him the lizard was lust. The angel offered to cut it off, if the man was willing. At first, he was not. Finally, the man let it go and said, "Cut if off." The angel did, and the lizard became a great horse, and the man's body changed, and he rode it to heaven.

Sally was praying about this strange story when she had the strong impression, "Lust is your problem." She was pondering this, "How can lust be my problem? I don't think about other men." While she was struggling with this, she received a message that Wayne was on the radio for her. When she heard his appeal to come to Wagu, she found herself resisting. Then, the impression came, "You have a lust for comfort." Suddenly, it all made sense. "Forgive me. Lord. Cut it [that nasty lizard]

213

off. I will go, but You will have to help me find people who will take the children." She needed to find families to care for the children because Jamey was too young and the window of time she would be in the village was too short for placement in the children's home. God provided volunteers to take the children, and Sally prepared to join her husband.

Sally was on the plane within a few days and went right to work nursing the flu victims in Wagu. A common destructive practice of the Bahinemo people at the time was to withhold water and food from people who were sick. Hydration is crucial to nearly every sickness in the tropics.

Sally administered easily-digested food and water. She also passed out liberal amounts of malarial medicine to address the secondary impact of malaria taking over after the flu weakened their immune systems. With this protocol, she was able to prevent the people in Wagu from dying of the flu. After a week or so of caring for them and preparing meals for Wayne and Bill, she became aware that she was no longer noticing the mosquitoes, the heat, and other discomforts because the lustful focus of her feelings was gone. She learned over the years after that experience that focusing on herself always stole her joy and her sense of peace with God.

The Wagu church tried to send aid to Yigai as well as food and medicine, but the head of the Yigai village rejected their food, and the majority of the villagers retreated into the jungle. Several more people from Yigai died before the epidemic was over.

Sally was back in Ukarumpa by mid-December when school was out, grateful to those who had taken Jamey and Tom. Wayne and Bill stayed on until a few days before Christmas to make sure the house was mosquito proof and livable for the children. They had actually intended to all go to Wagu to celebrate Christmas with the village, but they were short the funds for the flights. Extra money had come in from special donations to cover the initial costs of flights and equipment for the Wagu house, including a used generator and electric lights, but even with these extra funds, money was short, and they had to sell much of what they brought back with them from the US to pay for the return trip after Christmas.

Wayne had invited three volunteers to come to the village in January. They were in the AMFAM program, to be A Missionary For A Month, and were a great help with finishing details inside the house.

Sally was involved in the design of the birthing room in their house. She made sure it was set up with running water. The easy-to-clean cement floor sloped to a wide drain to catch all the birth fluids. A roof timber supported the trapeze-type rope the women clung to during final contractions. The men took on the challenge of walling the new birthing room off in one corner of the larger work room, including an inner door, in addition to the private outer door made in November. The wall and overhead frame were completed. However, they were unable to finish covering the wall with the traditional palm stems that day.

In the middle of the night, a woman in full labor awakened Sally seeking the room's privacy to give birth. Wayne and the three men got up at four in the morning and worked by battery-operated fluorescent lighting to finish the interior privacy wall. The first sound the young volunteers heard the next morning was the cry of a healthy newborn baby..

These men helped with many other practical projects to get the house functioning. Sally had heard ahead of time that one of these men, Harvey Wood, was a biology teacher, so she borrowed a microscope from Ukarumpa High

Left to Right - Harvey Wood, Howard Wilkins, Malcom Cocking, teaching about germs with a microscope.

school. Harvey helped show all the people who were interested the malaria larvae in the proboscis of mosquitoes. He found the malaria parasites in three out of four mosquitoes he put under the microscope, and he also found a strange amoeba with unusual cilia on its protrusions. He showed his findings to the Wagu people, helping them to begin to understand some of the causes of diseases. This understanding of disease-causing parasites helped increase their willingness to seek medicine when they were sick. Harvey continues to help the villagers by giving financial support to this day.

That spring, Sally started training six of the best readers to teach others how to read using the literacy materials she had been developing. Yafei and Kokomo were among the men and women who learned to read during that period.

Wayne and Sally wrote in their letter to their prayer partners in April of 1970:

"Our greatest joy came when the village leaders came to us and said, 'Now that we have built your house, you must get busy and translate God's Word for us. We are starving because so little of it is in our language. Don't you worry about going to the distant villages. We will go and tell them about God. That's our job. You must sit down and translate more food for our souls to grow on.'"

Yafei teaching others to read.

While Wayne and Sally did not really see it at the time, the changes in them and in the Wagu village culture were significant and positive. For Wayne and Sally, the new house and welcoming attitude of the people made Wagu a happy place to live and work. They went from dreading their time in the village to looking for ways to spend more time there. They allowed the children to have more freedom to play with the many new children in the village. Joy wrote to her friends about how fun the

Gwami. Kokomo and Kiawi. baptizing 38 Gahoms. Bitaras and village was. Those in the Wagu church enjoyed a new self-identity as children of God and brothers and sisters of Jesus. This identity had a profound impact on their approach to each other and their approach to the spirit world.

The church was growing during this time;, on successive weekends in May of 1970 the church leaders baptized a total of 38 people; some from Wagu, others from Gahom and Bitara. Edie and Joy were baptized at this time. The new village site had a gravelly beach, allowing them to wade into deep water and have the Baptisms right in front of the village. Wayne wrote to his mother that most of the village were now Christians.

The church leaders in general and Naba, Begai and Kokomo in particular began to make structural changes in the way they treated their wives. The Bible said to love their wives; they began to ask themselves what that meant. One big item was not objecting when their wives used towels or rags during their monthly periods to avoid being isolated in the mosquito-and-fly infested shack in the woods. It did not take long for other women to follow their example, and their monthly cycles no longer required their isolation.

Girl in a post church initiation ceremony: Left to right - Tawa, Lofu-kweli, Yaba, Bawi, Bayei, Sufa

Also during the spring of 1970, three young girls in the church came of age. The traditional girls' puberty ceremonies involved isolation, significant food restrictions, brutal whippings that left lifelong scars, and worship of the *wulyal* spirits. The church leaders eliminated all of those things, keeping only the community celebration dance to honor the young women. Some of the women from the previous initiation joined the group of honored women.

There were many other smaller changes that had a positive impact on their health and welfare, but some of the more structural impacts initiated by Begai, Naba, Kokomo, and the church leadership came through intentional changes that the church leaders talked through and passed out to the congregation.

Since the Bahinemos wanted to go out and witness, Wayne thought his translation team might be interested in how the first disciples had witnessed, so he started translating Acts. The first part drew their interest, but the situation was so different, they had difficulty identifying with the culture and situations. Wayne was about ready to set Acts aside until later, but Begai became excited at chapter 10, in the part about Peter's vision of all the forbidden animals in the sheet. Peter objected after he was told by the voice in the vision to eat the forbidden animals, *"'I have never eaten anything that our Jewish laws have declared impure and unclean.' But the voice spoke again, 'Do not call something unclean if God has made it clean'."* Begai connected with Peter's dilemma: Peter was facing food taboos from his old religion just as the villagers had food taboos in their old religion. God was telling Peter he must go ahead and eat those foods because God had declared them clean. Begai and the other leaders discussed this and decided to ask God to show them which tabooed foods they could eat at what times. Begai felt confident God would protect him from the *wulyal* who would be angry and try to hurt him. He excitedly shared this with others in the church service on Sunday. Others were hesitant. Eventually, all the Christians broke free of the taboos by faith that Christ would protect them from the *wulyal* spirits. Most unbelievers observed the result and broke the taboos as well.

Another area that changed significantly was the selection of brides. Traditionally, the clan had chosen the bride from another clan to bring peace between clans, but now there was increased freedom for young people to choose whom to marry.

The process of negotiating bride price also changed. At the first wedding among Christians, Begai excitedly told Wayne how peaceful and generous the exchange was. The villagers saw this as an incredible change for the better.

The change in polygamy was another area of transformation. In the past, powerful men frequently took multiple wives, leaving young single men without wives. Denominational churches they had contact with in Ambunti were strongly against polygamy. The Wagu church leaders were confused. Traditionally, someone in the clan was obligated to marry the widow of a clansman as a way to take care of her. In Wagu in 1964, six men had two or three wives, three men had one wife and ten men had no wife. Now they were hearing from Christians outside that they should even divorce second wives

They asked Wayne what they should do. He gathered together passages on marriage and divorce from the Old and New Testaments; and they translated them together. Then Wayne encouraged the leaders to pray and ask God to show them what

The village meeting in council to resolve conflicts.

to do. They returned and Begai stated their decision. "We do

221

not see that the Bible said polygamy is wrong, but we see it as selfish for one man to have several wives and others do not have any. We agreed on one rule for Wagu. 'No one can take a second wife until ever man has one'." This simply worded decision had a profound effect on marriage patterns that all saw as fair enough to override traditional cultural rules. By 1980 five men still had their original extra wives, sixteen men had one wife, four men did not have a wife and one older widow had not yet married.

Following Christ made a difference in how the village dealt with conflict. When the Dyes had arrived in Wagu in 1964, people yelled out their complaints so all in the village could hear. People then tended to take sides and escalate the conflict. Often this ended in blows. Yafei and Bagi ended up hitting each other with anything they could get their hands on. Sally had had to clean and tape up Bagi's head after one of their fights. A wife who was beaten or felt mistreated had a ritual crying pattern to call everyone's attention to her pain. After the people started meeting in 1968, the leaders called people together to discuss problems. By 1971 these discussions had developed into what amounted to a village court system. Village leaders would listen to the complaints and determine the measure of fault. Most of the village would sit around the circle, with women and children near the back. Interpersonal issues were often settled by exchanging money. Each would give according to the weight of their offense. Most issues were resolved within the village, sometimes ending with prayer.

However, some more extreme or repeated offenses were taken to the government officer in Ambunti.

Kokomo embraced the bible and allowed it to change many of his ideas. He went against his culture and began helping his wife with many jobs that were traditionally women's work including making sago. He helped in the raising of his kids and carried the heavy loads others would have their wives carry.

Waga helping his wife across the river - new behavior in Wagu

These pastors led by example and some change took place over night. Other changes took place over a number of years, and were not completely obvious. Wayne and Sally were often focused on the sick child in front of them, the broken canoe, the lack of progress on the translation, or the lack of money in the checking account. The truth was that the village of Wagu was beginning to thrive. There was food and clean water, the majority of children were living to grow up and realize their own dreams, and the fear of the *kwonu* was no longer the major driver of their lives. The Wagu church was growing, self-directed, seeking the Bible for guidance, sending out missionaries, helping its community cope with daily hardships of living. The church in Wagu was becoming the church that Wayne and Sally had imagined in their discussions back at the University of Michigan, a church like the one Wayne had witnessed during jungle camp in Mexico and wrote home about. Faith, hope and freedom had replaced fear, for both the people of Wagu and for Wayne and Sally.

Wayne, Sally, and their Bahinemo team translated large portions of the New Testament and helped nurture the Wagu church.

When Wayne and Sally returned from Michigan, Wayne took on the lead role in the anthropology committee. He and Sally began writing up some of the changes they were observing in Wagu and presenting those to the anthropology committee for discussion and as a way to learn what worked and what did not work.

These anthropology papers began to get circulated around the organization, and in 1973, the Executive Director of SIL International approached Wayne with a request to look at the issue of church growth across the whole of Wycliffe. Wayne and Sally accepted the assignment, and they began to study the results of Bible translation in fifteen programs in Mexico and the Philippines to see if there was a pattern for response to the translations in their languages. The research from these trips encouraged Wayne to get a doctorate in cross-cultural missiology from Fuller Theological Seminary. Missiology uses the insights from anthropology, sociology, psychology, and theology together to investigate the mandate, message, and mission of the Christian church, especially the nature of missionary work. Sally earned the degree Master of Arts in Missiology. She also completed all the core courses for Fuller's Marriage and Family Counseling

Master's program.

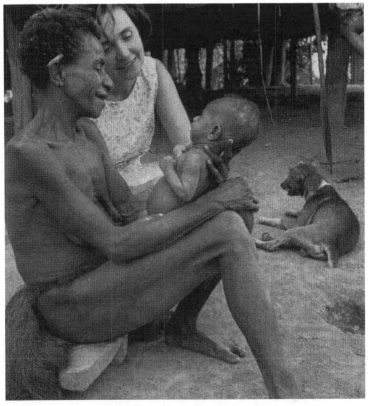

Sally and Yagumei admiring young Mathew, Yafei and Moyali's son

Wayne and Sally continued to work with the Wagu tribe on translation, education, and improvements to their medicine.

New Tribes mission had started a translation center in Menesuyo on the far side of Mt. Hunstein to translate the more isolated "Inaru language" undiluted by Tok Pisin in the early 1980s. They did not realize it was actually the Bahinemo language. Wayne and Sally eventually turned the Bahinemo program over to NTM. Most of the NTM missionaries left, but Jason and Toni Stuart persisted and completed the New Testament and part of the Old Testament.

Edie and Joy each stayed in the village one year after high school to teach the children to read Bahinemo and Tok Pisin using Sally's primers. When Begai became the provincial officer, he succeeded in establishing a government funded school in Wagu. A local government trained doctor joined the village and took over responsibility for medical care.

After the Bahinemo language program was turned over to NTM, Wayne and Sally were asked by the Eastern African Group of SIL to consider taking the role of Academic Coordinator for the six countries in that group. They would need to make a major move to Nairobi, Kenya. Before leaving, they made one last trip to Wagu to encourage the people and to say goodbye in 1989.

The village of Wagu grew in numbers and in the health of its people. Leaders from Wagu moved into local government roles, and school began to graduate some students who went and received high school diplomas from the regional government school in Wewak. They are now fully qualified teachers in Wagu School classrooms.

The Wagu people began to lose interest in the Bahinemo language and embrace Tok Pisin as the more progressive language to learn and teach their children. Since the government schools now require English, many in the younger generation can speak English.

An Assemblies of God preacher from Ambunti began to visit

regularly and a new church was started in Wagu.

Kokomo Teaching

When Sally and Jamey returned to the village in 2012 there was a renewed interest in preserving the language. There were two thriving churches, and the Wagu people were actively involved in the larger East Sepik Church. Jason Stuart with New Tribes Mission was the driver behind getting the Bible finished and was one of the main speakers at the dedication. It is interesting to note that Wayne's Uncle Cecil had been a founder of the mission that completed the translation Wayne and Sally started.

Kokomo was still mentoring young pastors and there was a large group of women active in worship, teaching, and bible study. These women were also going out on evangelistic trips and meeting with the churches in other communities up and down the river.

Jason and Toni helped establish a church in Inaru; the people of

227

Wagu helped establish a church in village of Gahom.

At the time of the publishing of this book the population of people living in the Gahom/Genesowayagu territory has increased to over 1000, most of whom are relatives of 308 "Gahoms" Wayne and Sally first met in 1964 through 1966.

In one of the last conversations we had with Kokomo before leaving in 2012, he said he was going to go to Inaru to help nurture the church there.

Yalfei's son Mathew runs a tourist guest house in Wagu. You can email him at Mathew Kaka

wagulake@googlemail.com.

You can also get more information at:

www.wagurainforest.com

There is more content, photos, letters, stories and essays at

www.wagurainforest.com

Note: Any proceeds from this book will be added to the funds provided by many individual and business supporters towards "The Bahinemo Fund", a non-profit organization that is dedicated to providing medical supplies, and education for the Wagu people and the communities in the east Sepik area.

Made in the USA
Columbia, SC
29 June 2017